LEADERSHIP BY CHOICE

7 Keys for Maximizing Your Impact
and Influence in the Workplace...
Right Where You Are

SUE SALVEMINI

LEADERSHIP BY CHOICE

7 Keys for Maximizing Your Impact and Influence in the Workplace...
Right Where You Are

 Capucia

Published by:
Capucia, LLC
211 Pauline Drive #513
York, PA 17402
www.capuciapublishing.com

ISBN: 978-1-945252-38-9
Library of Congress Control Number:

Cover Design: Ranilo Cabo
Layout: Ranilo Cabo
Editor and Proofreader: Gwen Hoffnagle
Book Midwife: Carrie Jareed
Photography: Stacey Hughes Photography *www.staceyhughes.com*
Website Design: Renee Dupuis *www.meadowbrookwebdesigns.com*

Printed in the United States of America

DEDICATION

**In honor and memory of my mother
Carol Ramsdell Boyajian
1935 – 2011
Whose inspiration, guidance, vision, and leadership
continue to impact and influence the world today.**

~

For teaching me to love, lead, and laugh – and laugh we did!
For sharing her values – unconditional love, dedication,
integrity, adventure, and fun.
For sharing her vision – a family filled with love,
laughter, openness, and warmth.
For her incredible attitude – the epitome of positive; and her
amazing ability to find the good in the bad and
the beautiful in the messy.
For her courage and strength – never allowing
anything to slow her down, especially when it came to her
family. She was the glue that bonded us.
For her passion to learn and live – getting her college degree
in her fifties, trying new recipes to share and crafts to make,
swimming for exercise, coffee for friendships,
and supporting her children's quests for the same.
For her never-ending praise and unconditional support –
she raised us up "so we could stand on mountains."
Lifting us up daily in all she did and said,
she believed in us when we couldn't.
For giving her heart and listening ears – she was *always* there
to listen, comfort, and offer advice when asked, and silence
when needed. She gave us unending space to be heard.

TABLE OF CONTENTS

Newton's Cradle

The first time I saw Newton's Cradle it was sitting atop my science teacher's desk in middle school. I was fascinated as he pulled one of the six balls up away from the others, released it, and watched it strike the next ball. Fully expecting all of the balls to move, I was curious to understand how the four middle balls stayed in place, yet the sixth, or end ball, moved an equal distance and in the same arc as the first, only to repeat the sequence as it returned and hit the balls again in the opposite direction, like a pendulum swinging. Both end balls moved yet the middle balls remained stationary. Despite no visible sign of impact, clearly something was happening between the two end balls that involved each ball in between.

The second time I saw Newton's Cradle was in my husband's third grade classroom. He used it to build his students' curiosity and to introduce them to Sir Isaac Newton's third law of motion:

For every action there is an equal and opposite reaction.

He then taught them how momentum and energy is transferred across the middle balls, demonstrated visibly by the action and movement of the two end balls, and that while there is no observable movement in the middle balls, they are impacted by the force created by the adjacent balls, transferring the energy back and forth between sequences.

The third time I saw Newton's Cradle was by design. In the days leading up to a workshop I was planning I shared the framework of my workshop with my husband, seeking suggestions for a visual model to best capture the message of leadership impact and influence. He immediately related my message to Newton's Cradle and the science behind it.

As a leader you are often the visible force represented by the leading ball of Newton's Cradle. You are the ball that starts the motion, creates momentum, and initiates a transfer of energy. Your force or energy is transferred sequentially from you to those around you. Just because you cannot always see your impact does not mean it is not being felt and transferred, as it is between the balls in Newton's Cradle. Your leadership, impact, and influence are the beginning of a transfer of energy, force, and momentum directly to those surrounding you. It is up to you to choose and create the impact you will have, embracing that regardless of what you may or may not observe, you are making a difference and influencing an action and reaction.

Thank you for choosing this book as part of your journey to being an exceptional leader. I am honored to be a part of your journey and humbled that you chose this book, truly!

The material and content in *Leadership By Choice* are a metamorphosis of years of learning, experiencing, reading, and growing. I was blessed to have had the amazing guidance of two phenomenal parents who taught me that I could do and be anything I could imagine, followed by a life of being surrounded by great leaders, mentors, family, and friends. I share some of the greatest lessons I have learned along the way that have contributed to my leadership development and journey. I experienced at an early age the honor of being a leader and the privilege it is to be trusted to work alongside a group of people, leading them to achieve a common goal. I have always taken the role seriously and know that because you are reading this book you also recognize the impact you can have in leadership roles as you strive to be "better."

Embrace this as an interactive book written to help you think. Throughout the book I ask you to take time to reflect and relate concepts to your own experiences. **To help you in this process I designed the *Leadership By Choice Reflection Journal* to accompany the book. You can download the journal at www.leadershipbychoice.com.** This journal is my gift to you so you can capture your thoughts while reading *Leadership By Choice* and keep them together in one place for your reference.

In addition to the prompts from the book, the journal includes additional reflection exercises to provide greater depth of experience. Your opportunity to grow and develop exists in the thought and reflection you apply to your personal situations, and is further deepened when you share them. In my workshops the greatest growth and "aha" moments have come when two or three people shared their thoughts and reflections with each other. I encourage you to foster an opportunity for the same by reading the book with a colleague or two and sharing your reflections. While it's important to write down your thoughts, you can experience even greater impact when you take the time to share them with someone and in turn listen to their reflections. Something magical happens when we articulate our thoughts with another, especially when we share common goals such as growing as leaders.

My vision is to help leaders like you have positive impact and influence in the workplace. If everyone embraces the honor of being a leader and the incredible opportunity to make a lasting difference, *everyone* benefits.

INTRODUCTION

My first real job was as a chambermaid at the Flying Cloud Motel in Laconia, New Hampshire, one summer at the age of twelve. I can still remember Lois training me in the proper way to make hospital corners and the value of polishing away the water spots on the stainless steel faucets in the bathrooms to make sure the patrons had a clean, shiny, pristine room to vacation in. She took time to work with me, develop my skill set, encourage me, and give me opportunities for career advancement by teaching me to manage the front desk and take reservations! While it was a short-lived career of two summer months, it was my first job with a paycheck, and whereby I had the opportunity to learn a set of skills, master them, and work among a team of fellow chambermaids doing the same. I experienced my first boss and gained incredible pride in independently spending my summer earnings on my eighth grade school wardrobe. I vividly remember the confidence I felt as I walked into my first day of school wearing my vibrant-yellow corduroy suit with a vest and gaucho pants, beautifully contrasted with a flaming rust-colored silk blouse!

Many years and jobs later (and clothing, thankfully), I have had the extreme pleasure of working with and for some inspirational leaders. I am humbled by all I have learned from them and for the leader I have grown to be, in large part as a result of their guidance, mentorship, and passion for their leadership roles. They treated the role of developing their teams as a privilege, a passion I adopted and passed on. I have also had the all-too-common experience of working for and around leaders who were less inspiring – who hadn't developed their leadership skills and lacked awareness of their ability to impact people for better or worse, the result being unhealthy work environments with high attrition rates, uneasiness, and stress.

In a 2013 study by *Harvard Business Review* it was revealed that executives, managers, and professionals spent on average 13.5 hours per day working during the work week and an additional five hours during their weekends. Assuming the average person strives for at least six hours of sleep per night, that leaves about 4.5 hours of non-working time each day. In other words, professionals spent 75 percent of their waking hours working. With the increasing and almost universal use of smartphones, many professionals rarely "tap out" of work, making job satisfaction that much more imperative. For many of you, this statistic is not surprising – you are living it!

Because you're reading this book, I'm guessing you're an "A player" – you take pride in yourself, your work, and your results. You value self-development and push yourself to be better, learn more, go the extra mile, find that extra pearl of wisdom, and improve your leadership skills along the way. You take pride in being your personal best at everything you do, including how you work with your colleagues and manage relationships. You hold yourself accountable at a very high level and expect the same of those around you. In fact you thrive on accountability and a sense of achievement!

As a result, you may find yourself frustrated when others do not view accountability and personal responsibility as you do, sometimes negatively impacting your ability to perform, produce, or reach your goals, which frustrates you even more. On the outside you maintain a calm demeanor, but your inside voice and thoughts say otherwise. You are not alone.

I recently read that a reported 80 percent of people do not love their jobs. They like and in some cases "love" the physical work they do, but often feel uninspired, underappreciated, or frustrated in their roles. Many relate the primary source of their job dissatisfaction to their immediate supervisor. They have a constant feeling of being overwhelmed with work and unclear about their direction in their profession. They are frustrated because they want to make a difference and want to understand their career path, but feel they cannot do so where they are.

Such reports have been further validated in my workshops and work as an executive leadership coach. My workshop attendees and clients are typically high-achievers and extremely successful individuals. They are deeply committed to their work, often navigating dual roles of leading their teams and being members of senior leadership or executive teams. Discussions revolve around common challenges they face at all levels, regardless of their positions. Many feel caught in the daily challenges of managing versus leading, performing the many requirements of their jobs, getting along better with colleagues and their immediate supervisors, and working on a team or in a company in which the direction is unclear and the style of leadership is challenging for them to embrace, let alone thrive and grow in. They experience an overabundance of work that requires far more hours than the workday provides, only to come back in the morning and experience the same thing the next day. After a certain amount of frustration they either accept their role and it becomes just a J-O-B that is hopefully paying the bills, or they believe that the problems are unique to the job or the organization and choose to find a new one. In both scenarios they become disengaged and less productive, spending most of their time thinking about what they would rather be doing. It doesn't have to be this way.

What would the world look and feel like if everyone loved their work? Imagine your alarm clock going off in the morning and you jump out of bed eager to embrace another day of work, headed to a job:

- You are passionate about
- That aligns deeply with your core values
- Where your vision is clear
- Among colleagues you respect, enjoy, and thrive around
- Where you embrace challenges with confidence
- Where your growth and development is encouraged
- Where you are valued and appreciated for your strengths, hard work, and commitment
- Where taking time for reflection, exploration, and idea-creation is part of the culture

Imagine wanting to grab your phone on the way home from work to call your spouse or closest friend and share the great work you are honored to be part of and the difference you know you are making. Imagine walking into your home with the energy and desire to pass on your feelings of accomplishment, fulfillment, and passion to those closest to you, and the same eagerness and energy to hear about their days.

Imagine that day.

Imagine that job.

Imagine the effect.

Now imagine this is going on in every home around you! What would it feel like to know that *you* are the person impacting and influencing this in others and in your culture and work environment – that you are the leader? What if I told you that you have this opportunity now, right where you are – would you believe me?

I believe you do have this opportunity, and I believe you can access all of this and more; because not only have I created this for myself, but I have also had the extreme privilege of working with and coaching others on this same journey.

Leadership By Choice is about recognizing that you already are a leader. But what does it mean to be a leader? If you were to research the definition, you would find hundreds. In fact there are as many different definitions of *leader* as there are leaders. For example, Google defines *leader* as a position often accompanied with a title:

The person who leads or commands a group,
organization or country.

Bill Gates defines *leaders* as empowering:

"As we look ahead into the next century, leaders will be those who empower others."

And John C. Maxwell defines a *leader* as a guiding example for others:

"A leader is one who knows the way, goes the way, and shows the way."

I define a *leader* as someone who has impact and influence, and I believe each of you has a unique opportunity to inspire, influence, and directly impact the productivity and lives of those who work for you and around you.

Leadership is the ability to create a vision, inspire and motivate yourself and others to move towards that vision, find opportunity in the obstacles along the way, and execute a plan to make the vision a reality. **Strong leaders are the key to creating powerful teams and exceptional organizations and are not restricted to a specific title.** Though your title might add to your prescribed or formal area of influence or reach, you do not need a title to lead and have influence. In *Leadership By Choice* I invite you to explore seven key areas at the heart of being a leader who has a positive impact, makes a lasting difference, and inspires greatness in others.

I have met many people who shared "what I hope to achieve when…" – when they are in a new position, when they lead a larger team, when this, when that… tomorrow or the next day. I wrote this book to help you reshape your passion about leadership *today*; to offer an opportunity to embrace what is right in front of you, *currently*; and to invigorate you to find the true joy in the work you currently do and make a lasting difference in the world *now*, right where you are.

I believe that in every moment and in every interaction you have the choice to influence, impact, and inspire others. The question is not *if* you will do this; the question is how you will *choose* to do this. What is your leadership choice?

I will share with you seven key leadership choices to maximize your impact and influence immediately. I will not tell you how to lead; I believe you have been perfectly designed and placed in your role. I also believe that being your authentic, uniquely qualified self is exactly what your team, your colleagues, and your organization need to be successful. *Leadership By Choice* is about helping you connect with the talents you already bring to the table – to hone in on them and maximize their impact and effectiveness in your workplace.

As a young second lieutenant in the Army, fresh out of college and ROTC, I was hardly prepared to be the platoon leader of a cable and wire platoon consisting of forty-eight men and women ranging in age from eighteen to thirty-seven! In the military you wear your title and accolades on your uniform, perfectly sewn on within millimeters of prescribed placement. As a result I quickly learned that the airborne paratrooper badge on my uniform elevated my status in the platoon. Under normal circumstances the arrival of a new platoon leader is quite similar to that of a new boss showing up. There is a time of evaluation, "checking out," assessing how this new figure will play a part in your job as your new boss, and determining whether they are qualified to lead.

While I was never overly obsessed about being the only female officer in my unit, I quickly learned that one way to earn the respect of my peers and junior-ranking enlisted personnel was to demonstrate strong physical fitness, courage, and boldness. Wearing the airborne patch demonstrated without any words or actions that I had qualified for and been accepted to Army paratrooper training and in so doing achieved a certain level of fitness excellence, participated in an aggressive training program, and jumped out of a perfectly good airplane a minimum of five times, including in the dark of the night – a feat many would not consider – in addition to successfully training and completing such a program. It is a badge that is highly respected in the Army, and to wear it as an officer – and a woman no less – immediately earned me a level of respect from the platoon. In wearing and displaying that badge I delivered a message of confidence, commitment, and willingness to push myself physically and emotionally, without ever saying one word.

In the civilian world of corporate America, once you're hired and your resume is filed, you have no badge to represent the accomplishments of your past – no visual reminders pinned to your suit. The only badge you wear is your daily activity. Your daily actions, language, attitude, and presence *are* your badge. You have a choice each day, each moment: How will you show up? How will you lead? How will those around you be impacted by your presence – positively or negatively? How will you enhance the working environment? Will you breathe life into your colleagues or dampen it and take it away? You choose. I invite you to join me in exploring how you can maximize your impact and influence in the workplace, today, right where you are!

Reflection Exercise 1:

What inspires you about being a leader?
What do you hope to gain from reading this book?
Describe your ideal job.

Download the Journal at: www.leadershipbychoice.com

PART I

The Force: Start with You

Your ability to lead others starts with how
you choose to lead yourself.

CHAPTER 1

Embrace Your Values

Life isn't about waiting for the storm to pass...
it's about learning to dance in the rain.
— Vivian Greene

I felt the snap. Followed by a loud crunch and a pulsating wave of pain that travelled from my right foot up through my calf to my entire leg, landing deep in the gut of my stomach. As I gulped in air to get my breath, I gingerly limped over to my left to remove myself from the path of 2,000 eager half-marathoners on this perfectly beautiful fall day on the Northshore of Massachusetts — this sunny and crisp, fifty-two-degree, perfect running-weather day. There we were, my sixteen-year-old son ahead of me in the faster pack, running our first half-marathon. I had seen this day in my head for weeks while training, visualizing crossing the finish line, seeing the medal placed around my neck, my heart smiling from the knowledge that I had conquered and accomplished something I never thought my body could handle, gleaming at the joy of knowing that our son would achieve this milestone in his life at such an early age. I had seen the victory and felt the overwhelming personal joy. I had lived what was going to happen in approximately two hours. So I thought.

I held back the nausea from the pain and shock while I blindly limped and wrestled with what I subconsciously knew had happened. Somewhere in the midst of my blaring running soundtrack my inner voice screamed, "You just broke your foot!"

"No way," I argued back. "There is NO WAY – it is mile one and I still have twelve more to go. I have trained for this for weeks."

"Call Tom, let him know."

"No! I have to figure this out. Maybe it isn't broken. Maybe it was a knot in my foot that just released. Ahh, that's it! Maybe I can walk the race. After all, when I made the decision to do this race I promised myself that even if I had to run/walk it, it would still be an accomplishment, one I privately contemplated for years."

Limping along, putting weight only on the back edge of my heel, I considered my choices. A fellow runner came alongside me, put her hand on my shoulder, and mouthed, "Are you okay?!" Unable to hear her, as my "focus and run" praise music was still playing loud enough to block out all noise, I lifted my head, smiling and beaming; thanked her; and without a second thought assured her I would see her at the finish line even if it meant I had to crawl! As the words flowed from my mouth I recognized that I had made my choice. I would be leading myself to the finish line; I just wasn't quite sure how.

When you find yourself faced with a decision – a moment to choose between two options, a moment when the timing seems imminent – how do you make your selection? Do you refer to a list of predefined rules? Do you dig into your gut, your heart, your core? Or do you just do it and not really think about why or how?

In order to maximize your impact and influence in the workplace, you must understand *why* you do what you do and how your work aligns with your core values.

Reflection Exercise 2:

Why do you do the work you do?

Download the Journal at www.leadershipbychoice.com

Core Values

Core values are defined as the fundamental beliefs of a person or organization. In an organization they represent the heart of its guiding principles and what the organization and employees stand for. These values are often stated in the organization's mission statement, and are usually the basis for defining and developing the corporate culture and fundamental operating decisions.

On a personal or individual level, they represent deeply held beliefs – your highest priorities and fundamental driving forces or inspiration. They are the foundational guiding principles that direct your personal decisions, direction in life, and relationships.

At face value the definition of *core values* may seem the same whether organizational or individual; however, there is one major difference. Most organizations work diligently to identify them, publish them, and refer to them when making decisions, and individuals do not. I have found that people believe they innately understand their core values, demonstrated by simply living them day by day. And while being guided by them on a conscious and subconscious level, they are rarely documented in writing, reviewed for consistency, or systematically consulted in decision-making. It's time to change that.

After serving in the military I was blessed to start my corporate experience in sales at Johnson & Johnson, one of the world's largest and most successful pharmaceutical, consumer-goods, and medical-device companies in the world. For almost twenty years I directly experienced working for a company dedicated to honoring the core values created by the founders and outlined in the J&J Credo. The Credo is displayed on the walls of every J&J subsidiary company, found on page one of their annual report, and featured as the primary document in the "About J&J" section on their website. As "The values that decide our decision-making," the J&J Credo is a living, breathing, active representation of the core values, culture, and direction of J&J: "Our Credo is more than just a moral compass. We believe it's a recipe for business success."

Divided into four areas, the Credo represents the company's commitment to its customers, employees, communities, and stockholders, in that order. To ensure the company is accountable to upholding and maintaining the values outlined in the Credo, every employee participates in an annual Credo Survey. Multiple components about the company – including, for example, product development, product performance, customer experiences, employee performance and experience, and leadership direction and quality – are measured against the Credo in detail and evaluated from the perspective of every employee. The results are compiled and openly shared with everyone in the organization. As a manager in the organization, one of my top priorities was to lead and align my team's decision-making with the Credo. We were unified by a common set of core values and held accountable to lead in the same way. **When employees are aligned and clear on the organizational values, collaboration and decision-making become easier.**

Conflict Is the Result of Conflicting Values

Value-based decision-making provides a reference point for J&J and will do the same for you on a personal level. Identifying and aligning with your core values is powerful and helps you strategically in your decision-making. Once you truly understand them you will be surprised by the peace you have gained. Your ability to evaluate challenging decisions and weigh options of significant events dramatically improves. You shift and yield a greater sense of win-win versus lose-lose when you make challenging choices. Even trivial decisions are easier to make when you are able to align them with your values.

This concept came alive for me about two years ago on a personal level. I was struggling with what felt like a major decision about our upcoming family vacation and the possible financial investment we would need to make. It hit me like a ton of bricks when our oldest son turned fourteen: We only had four more years before he would be graduating from high school and most likely heading away to college. Our family of five would be changing, and the thought of having only four more summers to vacation together with our three teenagers landed a sense of urgency deep in my soul to plan meaningful and memorable family vacations.

Of course I knew that we would and could vacation together for many years after his graduation, but at that moment I wasn't thinking that way. All I could think about was that family time and vacations needed to be moved up on the priority list. Although we spent most of our weekends and school breaks together, the time was divided between attending various sporting events for our kids and trips to upstate New York to see extended family, and we often had to divide and conquer conflicting schedules. With three children in three different schools, and my husband teaching in yet another school, we were on four different school-year schedules, leaving summer months as our only time to schedule a bona-fide vacation together.

The first summer after my revelation about having only four family vacations left, we did our first ten-day trip to Utah to see and experience the national parks. It was a dream come true. In my entire working career the only other time I had taken more than a five-day vacation had been for my honeymoon almost twenty years prior!

So now it was summer number two with only two left to go before graduation. What to do? My husband and I found an amazing opportunity to live aboard a sailboat for one week in the Bahamas with just our family and the captain. Being avid scuba divers and eager to share this experience with our kids, we were beyond jazzed at the thought of taking this family trip. And surely it would be memorable. As a sailor, I couldn't imagine a better way to spend a week with my family – out on the ocean, kids learning to sail, snorkeling, scuba diving, playing cards, playing games, reading, and laughing – just the five of us and a captain who seemed like a great guy over the email communications. The price for the week was reasonable, which was also important, as we valued being financially responsible and not overextending ourselves. This trip couldn't be any more perfect!

Perfect… until we went to book the airline tickets. Between the price of the tickets and the additional nights of lodging needed because of limited flights to the island, the "reasonable" week on the sailboat tripled.

The decision felt impossible. Both choices offered a benefit, yet also contained a consequence. For weeks we wrestled with our choices: creating an amazing, memorable family vacation at the expense of being financially responsible, or being financially responsible and passing up this picture-perfect vacation. We could feel the wind and see the smiles on our kids' faces in anticipation of this unique and beautiful experience. Should we go for it and spend money we really didn't have in our vacation budget, possibly feeling guilty along the way; or should we save the money, desperately regretting our choice not to go? It felt like a lose-lose decision no matter what we chose. I equally wanted to choose both options and hated that I couldn't. Fortunately for me I was experiencing this dilemma at the same time I volunteered to participate in a "live" example for a group coaching call as part of my Institute for Professional Excellence in Coaching training.

As I reflect on this now, the struggle seems trite; but I can assure you there was a lot of emotion behind this decision, as in many challenges we face. At that moment the decision seemed critically important and tied to a highly emotional and deeply ingrained set of values. It was a decision that impacted our family and our sacred and coveted time together – time we felt was running out.

During the group coaching call my coach boldly asked me to share my dilemma and which values were in conflict. Up to that point I had never given my values much thought other than that they steered my daily decisions on a subconscious level. And I certainly hadn't related a conflict in values to this particular situation. I only knew that both my husband and I were genuinely struggling to make a decision we could live with.

My coach had me dig deeper into the conflicting values of creating memorable family vacations and being financially responsible. After several additional questions and deeper reflection, I came to realize that the value of creating memorable family vacations was more than that; it was about spending time together, independent of any location or venue. It suddenly seemed so clear, so simple. It was a bit embarrassing to acknowledge during the live training call how stuck I had been on a deep level, unable to see any sensible alternative solution I could embrace. The deeper, overriding core value was about being with my family and experiencing each other's company, and that did not require a cost-prohibitive trip. Suddenly I felt empowered by my epiphany and eager to focus my energy on our time together rather than on the location or cost. To further help me embrace my revelation, we concluded the training with me stating, "I am choosing to honor my value of spending quality time with my family over our vacation destination, and in so doing I am also honoring our value of being financially responsible." As soon as I released the specific sailing vacation and turned my focus towards spending quality time together, I was able to open my mind up to multiple opportunities and ways to accomplish this. It felt like "win" existed in our final choice.

Use Core Values to Guide Decision-Making

The shift was powerful, and from this experience I learned four valuable lessons:

1. When feeling conflicted about a choice, take time to examine the values behind the competing choices. Dig deeper to understand the overriding values that are in conflict, and don't assume that the initial value you embraced (such as memorable family vacations) is the overriding value (such as being with family and experiencing each other's company).

2. Once you understand the deeper core values that are in conflict, decision-making is easier. You choose to honor one value slightly more than another *equally important* value, not at the exclusion of it.

3. Once you transition from feeling that both choices are bad, your mind opens up to multiple options that honor both values, liberating feelings of win-win across the board!

4. By incorporating the language of choice – "I am *choosing* to honor my deeply held value of…" – you become empowered. In the example above, I didn't give the

amazing sailboat vacation another thought (at least for that summer) and had zero regrets, as the choice we made aligned with our overriding core values.

The language of *choosing to honor* empowered me in that moment and has since affected almost all of my decisions, as it will yours. It has been so transformational for me in evaluating both simple and complex decisions that I now incorporate this concept into most of my workshops and coaching. The results have been resounding.

Similar to Johnson & Johnson and many other companies that rely on their core values to guide them in value-based decision-making, you can incorporate this practice into your personal and professional life.

Discover Your Core Values

Uncovering your core values requires some thought and reflection. Below are four approaches to help you with this process:

The Brainstorming Approach

Brainstorming is a process that uses spontaneous thinking to generate creative ideas and solutions to problems. An individual or group records each thought that is generated without judgment, bias, or critique. When brainstorming as a group, a whiteboard or large poster paper is often used so everyone can consider the ideas together. Once all the ideas are captured, the individual or group further develops each idea for consideration.

If I asked you to spontaneously share your top five values with me right now you might pause and then rattle off some values that come to the top of your mind based on your current situation and emotions. At the moment mine would be:

- Family
- Harmony
- Hard work
- Faith
- Humor

The list seems fairly straightforward and it was pretty easy to quickly come up with some values that work for me. Though the true spirit of brainstorming is to generate thoughts without pausing to evaluate them or judge the process, if I were to spend just a few more minutes thinking about this list I might be alarmed at the order in which they easily flowed from my pencil, question if the order holds a deeper meaning or significance, and discover that I want to add additional values:

- Dedication
- Loyalty
- Fitness
- Timeliness
- Responsibility

Now it would feel a bit better, but still be missing some other values that are important to me:

- Financial responsibility
- Adventure
- Fun

This could go on for quite some time, but it's a good start! Try it for yourself and see what comes up for you. This brainstorming approach allows you to think freely without prompts or suggestive terminology. It is a great way to identify the values that consciously and subconsciously guide you – values that you at first define as your core values. As you review your list you might notice that your values have differing relevance depending on how you compartmentalize your life. For example, adventure and fun might be priorities for you in your personal life, but not at work, while hard work and timeliness take priority on the job. There are no right or wrong answers; getting at the core of your values helps you intentionally incorporate value-based decision-making into your life for peace of mind and productivity.

The Values-List Approach
Another way to approach identifying your values is to choose from a list of common values. It can be helpful to see the words in front of you rather than trying to identify them from a void. I use the following list with my clients and guide them to highlight whichever ones speak to or resonate with them, with the freedom to add any values not listed. Take a moment to mark those values that best describe what is important to you.

Accomplishment	Credibility	Health	Privacy
Accountability	Decisiveness	Honesty	Productivity
Achievement	Dedication	Humility	Professionalism
Adaptability	Dependability	Humor	Quality
Advancement	Development	Impact	Recognition
Adventure	Determination	Independence	Relationships
Affection	Discipline	Individuality	Relaxation
Ambition	Diversity	Influence	Reliability
Appreciation	Education	Innovation	Resilience
Attractiveness	Efficiency	Inspiration	Resourcefulness
Authenticity	Empathy	Integrity	Respect
Autonomy	Encouragement	Intelligence	Responsiveness
Balance	Endurance	Intimacy	Safety
Belonging	Enjoyment	Intuition	Security
Boldness	Enthusiasm	Joy	Selflessness
Calmness	Environmentalism	Kindness	Service
Candor	Ethics	Knowledge	Simplicity
Capability	Excellence	Leadership	Spirituality
Challenge	Fairness	Learning	Spontaneity
Charity	Faithfulness	Love	Stability
Cheerfulness	Family	Loyalty	Status
Cleanliness	Fearlessness	Motivation	Strength
Collaboration	Fidelity	Nature	Structure
Commitment	Financial	Open-mindedness	Success
Communication	responsibility	Optimism	Teamwork
Community	Fitness	Organization	Thoughtfulness
Compassion	Flexibility	Partnership	Timeliness
Competition	Freedom	Passion	Trustworthiness
Confidence	Friendship	Patience	Uniqueness
Connections	Frugality	Peace	Versatility
Consciousness	Fun	Perfection	Vision
Control	Grace	Performance	Wealth
Cooperation	Gratitude	Perseverance	Well-being
Courage	Happiness	Playfulness	Wisdom
Creativity	Harmony	Preparedness	Work Ethic

Categorize Your Values for Clarity

Review your identified values from either the brainstorming or the values-list approach and look for common themes. You may find that your values are easier to clarify by creating groups of values that represent a common theme or specific area in your life that is important to you. The categories possibly represent your core values better than the actual values themselves.

My composite list:

- Family
- Harmony
- Hard work
- Faith
- Humor
- Dedication
- Loyalty
- Fitness
- Timeliness
- Responsibility
- Financial responsibility
- Adventure
- Fun

When reviewing my values from the above exercise as a composite list, I immediately see the categories that lurk behind them that would not necessarily be obvious to someone else. It is clear that there are four important categories in my life and that some of my values, such as family, responsibility, and adventure, appear in more than one category:

- Family: family, adventure, fun, loyalty

- Faith: harmony, faith, dedication, responsibility, adventure

- Work: hard work, timeliness, responsibility, financial responsibility, adventure

- Health: family, hard work, fitness, adventure, fun

A single value can have multiple interpretations. For example, one person might value abundance using the financial interpretation of the word, while another might value abundance using the spiritual interpretation of the word. By grouping values together in categories that are important to you, you further define the relevance and interpretation of the core value for you.

Reflection Exercise 3

Using either the brainstorming approach or the values-list approach, identify your core values.

Download the Journal at: www.leadershipbychoice.com

The Situational-Analysis Approach

Another way to uncover your values is to reflect on your personal experiences. Rather than referring to a generic list of values, explore specific situations when you experienced a range of emotions. Through a simple analysis you will uncover your core values. The situations might include:

Conflict: Reflect on a time when you felt truly conflicted or genuinely stuck between choices, similar to the experience I shared about my vacation choice. Chances are you were stuck between values of significance to you.

Happiness: Think of times in your life when you felt incredibly happy, fulfilled, satisfied, accomplished, or at peace. Reflect on what it was about that time that brought you feelings of happiness. Lurking in and around those experiences are your core values.

Hot Buttons: Think of what really sets you off – pushes your buttons, frustrates you. Your values are hiding there as well.

Here is an example of how you can challenge yourself in a situation to uncover your true core values, as one of my clients did:

"Charles would rush in late for every single team meeting and make quite a scene, apologizing for being late again, and then using his phone or laptop for the bulk of the meeting," my client shared. "I hate tardiness and that he never contributes," he went on to explain.

"What values of yours would you say are being challenged?" I asked.

"Well, punctuality and timeliness. And respect for the rest of us."

"What is it about Charles specifically that is setting

you off?"

"We need him to be present and involved with this project. He is the brains in this, and showing up late and then doing his own thing is not helping us."

"In terms of values, are there any others that come to mind as you think about this situation?"

Silence for a moment, then: "Well, yes – teamwork and collaboration. Now that I think of it, I don't really even care if he's late – I just care that he is an active, contributing member of the team."

"So what specifically about your value of timeliness is being challenged?"

"Well, while I thought it was timeliness, I guess it really isn't. I just want to feel that he's engaged and committed to the team."

When identifying your core values, subordinate values often come up first, as they did for my client in the story above. Challenge yourself by asking what specifically about the event, action, or value gets to the essence, or core, of what was really bothering you or what was really making you happy. You might be surprised by what is revealed.

Reflection Exercise 4

Reflect on situations as outlined above to uncover additional core values.

Download the Journal at: www.leadershipbychoice.com

The Reflections-On-Your-Funeral Approach

Set aside some time for this last approach. Find a quiet, comfortable place, or go somewhere inspiring outdoors, and reflect more deeply about the values you identified above. You will benefit the most from this reflection time by journaling your thoughts or dictating them to a recording device.

Imagine that you have learned you have a limited time to live and are approaching the end of your life. You have decided to prepare your funeral. All of your family, relatives, friends, and colleagues from present and past work will be there. Several random acquaintances will be there too – the mechanic who repairs your car, the person who serves you coffee every morning, the receptionist at your doctor's office, and others like those. You must choose five people – a family member, a relative or close friend, a supervisor, a co-worker, and one of your casual acquaintances – to share their thoughts about you at your funeral. While you will not be present to hear what they say, you have an idea. Write down or dictate what you hope they will say about you. In a separate thought, add what you honestly believe they would say about you.

As you read what you have written (or listen to your dictation), what values are revealed in your descriptions of what you *hope* they will say? What values are revealed in what you *believe* they will say? Within the two lists is the essence of what you value most.

Reflection Exercise 5

What values do you discover as you reflect on how people would describe you at your funeral?

Download the Journal at: www.leadershipbychoice.com

Create a Personal Values Checklist

Feel free to use any of the four approaches to identify your core values. Record them as the founders of Johnson & Johnson did decades ago in their Credo. Your Personal Values Checklist should include your core values that you will now refer to when making decisions. When you make decisions, review your list to get a sense of which values influence your decisions the most. Accept that your list will change as your priorities change. For example, a colleague of mine valued his performance at work tremendously. And while he also valued his health and fitness, they often took second place when he was working on a major deadline. After a visit to the hospital and the scare of a possible heart attack, his value of fitness moved into first place and his routine changed as a result. Regardless of approaching deadlines he chose to make time every morning for a thirty-minute cardiovascular workout.

What is important in this exercise is to understand the values guiding you and driving you right now, so that you can recognize them when they are being challenged, are causing conflict, or need to be referred to for decision-making, and put them into action.

Reflection Exercise 6

Create a Personal Values Checklist.

Download the Journal at: www.leadershipbychoice.com

Value-Based Decision-Making

Your ability to lead yourself and others is easier when you can clearly refer to your core values when faced with conflict and making decisions. Just as the J&J Credo serves as a metric against which to measure critical decisions and practices, your core values can provide direction and reference points for your choices, motivation, endurance, and drive. Your core values act as a resource to guide your thinking and consideration. By identifying and embracing the values you choose to honor, your ability to intentionally lead and motivate yourself is empowered.

Below are some examples of real applications of this principle from clients. Note that "conflicting values" are as the client defined them for their situation.

Client 1

Situation / Decision Point: A senior executive breadwinner contemplating either taking a lower-paying job with a minimal commute and closer to her increasingly busy household with two young teenagers, or staying in her current role that comes with an extensive commute that keeps her away from her family for an extra two to three hours a day

Conflicting Values: More Time with Family versus Financial Stability

Choice and Positioning: "I have chosen to honor my value of fostering quality time with my girls at this point in my career, and will work on creative solutions to continue to maintain financial stability. This teenage time is critical, and now that I have reflected on it I feel great about my choice!"

Client 2

Situation / Decision Point: A senior executive in a stable and lucrative job contemplating taking a new job with a promotion in title and geographic responsibility but with significantly lower pay and no long-term guarantee or promise

Conflicting Values: Financial Stability versus Fun, Travel, Growth, and Development

Choice and Positioning: "I am honoring my value around always seeking growth and professional development above financial stability – and some fun and travel right now. In the end I feel a strong sense of 'win' with this opportunity in front of me, even if it is significantly lower in compensation. This new job will provide an opportunity to push myself to the next level of leadership."

Client 3

Situation / Decision Point: An articulate and bright office administrator who wants to move up in the organization but doesn't want to ask her boss about it, knowing that if she did move up her boss would be "high and dry" without her

Conflicting Values: Self-Advocacy and Growth versus Loyalty to Boss

Choice and Positioning: (In dialogue with boss): "I am conflicted about coming to you because I believe in loyalty and in supporting you. However, if I don't talk to you about this I would be ignoring another value equally important to me, which is advocating for myself." (A productive dialogue was initiated and a strategy amenable to both was put in place.)

Client 4

Situation / Decision Point: A division sales manager who worked long days repeatedly walked into her house to find the sink loaded with dirty dishes, wondering if anyone in the house cared at all about having a clean sink other than she.

Conflicting Values: Harmony in the Household versus Cleanliness and Order

Choice and Positioning: "I am choosing to honor harmony by happily cleaning the sink… again, which also honors my love for cleanliness!" (She privately shared that it brought her great humor when she repeated this chant to herself. The sink situation – I kid you not – comes up frequently, regardless of gender, with conflicting values ranging from those above to Respect, Collaboration, Responsibility, Selflessness, etc. It truly could be the next book!)

Client 5

Situation / Decision Point: An executive running her first half-marathon, which she has visualized completing for months while training, suddenly injures her foot in the first mile and struggles with what to do

Conflicting Values: Conquering Adversity versus Well-being

Choice and Positioning: "I am choosing to honor my insatiable drive to overcome adversity and obstacles and live out the vision in my heart slightly above my well-being."

Now that you have a baseline, I encourage you to challenge yourself on a daily basis to better understand how your values influence the work, thoughts, and feelings you experience. Lead yourself on a journey towards greater empowerment and confidence in your decision-making. If you are like many of my clients you will quickly realize the powerful difference that choosing to align with your core values makes in your ability to lead yourself.

When you conduct yourself in alignment with your core values, choices become clearer, decisions become easier, and you create opportunities for greater peace as you navigate challenging options. This same principle applies to leading others. When you understand the core values of those you work with you maximize your ability to provide leadership that they can relate to at the deepest value – their core.

Reflection Exercise 7

APPLICATION: How will you incorporate a deeper understanding of your values into having greater impact in your workplace today?

Download the Journal at: www.leadershipbychoice.com

CHAPTER 2

Feel Your Vision

The only thing worse than being blind is having sight but no vision.
— Helen Keller

"Sue, I have to admit it, I am feeling a bit unmotivated these days," reluctantly shared my client, a former senior-vice-president in her mid-fifties who recently "retired" from a prestigious financial institution. *"I have broken oaths to myself to get up early and follow a routine. I must say, I have had no problem learning how to relax! It's hard for me to believe that after working such a routine for years, I really have learned how to relax. But I have a lot to do to launch my new coaching business — my website, some additional training, follow-up with one of my clients. Oh, and I think the interview went well — looks like a go so I should be consulting soon there..."*

She continued for thirty-five minutes sharing the broad range of her tasks, obligations, and many to-dos that she clearly had no energy for. As she spoke, I heard an unemotional transfer of all that was in her brain of tasks she wanted to do to support her new business – tasks she normally would do without thinking twice, yet she was truly stuck about what could possibly be getting in her way. As a highly successful individual who achieved anything she put her mind to and who rarely suffered from lack of motivation, she was clearly facing a speed bump and couldn't figure it out, but knew it was bad – it was holding her back from achieving her goal of launching her new business, the very reason for her early "retirement."

Just uttering the words "I'm stuck" was like a knife in her gut – I could hear it as she reluctantly admitted this to me. She could barely even say the words, as if by verbalizing them she was claiming them as true – a truth she was feeling and desperately trying to find a way around. She even thought she might be feeling fear – another new emotion for her – about all she didn't know about running her own business, but curiously, she shared, this type of feeling had never slowed her down in the past. When she finally stopped to breathe for a quick second, I reminded her that it was natural to experience new emotions when pursuing a major life change, and then I gently asked her, "Tell me what your business looks like?"

"What do you mean?" she asked.

"What does it LOOK like – this business you are creating? Describe the people you are working with. Describe what you do each day. How are you meeting your clients? At the end of your day, how are you feeling about your work?"

Silence.

"In other words, what is your vision? WHY do you want to do this? When you first got the idea about this type of business, what was it that inspired you to want to change careers? What is it about this business idea that you can see and feel? I think you're stuck because you're going through the motions you believe are necessary, but you don't really know why you are doing it or where you are headed. When you have a job you go to every day, it is relatively easy to just get up and go, per se – it is part of your commitment, your responsibility, your routine. You simply do without giving it much extra thought. However, when you are in between as you are, or not sure what your job actually looks like, it can be hard to get up and go."

More silence. I wondered if I'd lost her. She had never been this quiet during a call. Softly she shared, "I'm not sure what that is, my job I mean. I'm not sure I truly know what it looks like. I've never really thought about it that way."

"Your vision is unclear. I believe that if you take time to imagine yourself in one year looking back on the year, you will start to SEE what it is you are trying to create, what you hope to be feeling and experiencing, and then you will know what you are working towards and what it will feel like as you achieve it! In essence, you will start to create your vision."

That was on a Friday. On Saturday morning my phone rang. She called me in tears. "Sue, I wanted to email you, but I couldn't put this in words. You need to know that yesterday's call was powerful. I had the biggest aha moment! Sue, you were right, I had no vision! I don't know if I have ever had a vision, but I have always been able to get up and go to work without giving it much thought. Now that I am on my own, I had no idea. I think I never thought about it because it required me to think about my feelings. You know I am not an emotional person. In fact, I have spent most of my career in finance taking pride in the fact that I am not an overly emotional person. It has been my strength to be able to keep my emotions at bay – I HAD *to get off the phone yesterday because I couldn't control my emotions. As I truly dug deep and thought about my vision – my desires, hopes, dreams, my "why" I went into this profession to begin with – I couldn't control my emotions. I don't even know if I am explaining myself now. All I can tell you is that when I quietly thought about your questions and forced myself to imagine my days, my work, and my life in one year, I became completely overwhelmed with emotion, dreams, and yes, vision. And now my vision is clear! I know WHY I want to do this! Thank you for helping me see what I couldn't see."*

See the Future

This is not a unique story. Many of those I work with have never contemplated a personal vision. Rarely do I meet people who have created a personal vision, experienced the power of having such a vision, and incorporated it into their daily routines. While they might work for an organization that has a vision or mission they embrace, they have never taken time to personalize a vision for themselves. It was in one of my first workshops designed for an elite group of senior executive women that I learned how rare it is for professionals to genuinely plan their professional journey; to actually think ahead one to five years and then work backwards in planning their career path. In a select group of eight, only two had ever done this. And of the two, only one had done so within the previous five years.

Many workshops later, with diverse participants of both genders and various professional roles and levels, my findings were the same. Less than 1 percent had ever consciously entertained answering the questions "Where do I see myself in one year?" and "Where do I see myself in five years?" It was in my workshops that they first tried to answer these questions about their future, and while some often *thought* it would be a good thing to consider, it was for no reason other than the busyness of their lives that they had never taken the time to actually do so.

You likely get into a car each work day to get to a predetermined destination. You know the place and what it looks like. You know approximately how long it takes to get there. There's a route, maybe there are alternate routes you use when needed, and you certainly know when you have arrived. If you didn't, you would still be driving aimlessly, wondering where you are going and never sure if you have arrived.

Trying to work a career or life without having established some sense of where you would like to be – a vision for yourself – can leave you wandering aimlessly and endlessly, wondering if you have arrived or where you were headed to begin with. Take some time to think deeply about what you want for your future. As you gain clarity and definition around that vision of where you want to go, you might decide to orchestrate your time and days differently. You might find that the route you are taking needs to be better navigated to ensure you reach your destination more precisely.

If you are like most of the professionals I have worked with, your time is already consumed with balancing many balls: career, family, activities, service, fitness… you name it – you are simply swamped just living each day, let alone taking time to really think through where you see yourself in one to five years. You simply don't have time to take on a task such as this, and if you did have the time, you still might not be able to envision what you want your future to look like or even where to begin. Or, like my client, you might be hesitant to deeply reflect on your core desires, hopes, and dreams.

This question often first poses itself when you're faced with a possible career change, whether due to something outside of your immediate control or a personal desire for something different. Sofia, a young woman I have mentored through the years but who is still at the beginning of her career and journey, recently called me when she was considering a job change. While she enjoyed her work as a marketing associate in a fast-paced, growing medical device company, she felt stalled in her career. She felt disconnected from her immediate supervisor and didn't think there was much opportunity to grow and develop under his leadership. She felt disengaged, and spent a lot of time dreaming about what might be next rather than focusing on her current job. Her interests in possible next jobs were all over the board, and she was exploring everything from sales and marketing for a start-up designer shoe company to an advanced role in upstream marketing for a different medical device company, which would require relocation across the United States. She was exploring a variety of job postings online ranging in scope and responsibility, noticing her diverse areas of interest. Feeling "all over the board," she wasn't sure how to proceed, and called me to seek some guidance.

Like most of those I speak with on this very topic, she really didn't have any idea what she wanted to do, let alone where she saw herself in one year. She just knew that something was missing, and her goal was to find her next role, as something needed to change.

Views from Different Angles

I explained two approaches to help Sofia gain clarity towards achieving the change she felt she desperately needed. Each approach offered her slightly different perspectives, or angles, from which to ultimately weave together her thoughts about exactly what a change might look like and to clarify exactly what she was trying to achieve:

Random and Spontaneous: One approach is purely random, embracing the goal of changing your job to whatever seems and feels best at the moment. You can review diverse and multiple job postings, "trying them on" to see which ones feel like potential fits based on your skill set, the company culture, and the work itself, and draw from that a framework of what you might like to do. I advised Sofia to identify specific aspects of the positions that appealed to her, make note of them, and ultimately create a picture of what she wanted her next job to look like, ultimately finding one that simply seemed and felt right for her at the moment.

Directed and Intentional: An alternative approach is to establish where you want to be professionally and personally in one to five years. This approach also encourages you to "try it on" and imagine what it would look like if you had a specific job, but to work backwards in planning your directional steps to get there. To do so you must jump ahead and review the past as if it had already occurred. I provided some specific prompts and exercises, and Sofia was able to better define what was important to achieve and what goals she connected with. This allowed her to create a vision and work towards achieving that vision in a directed and intentional manner.

Try It On

Both approaches require you to be able to "try it on" to see and feel what you are considering. Before you purchase a new piece of clothing, you usually try it on. In the dressing room you have an opportunity to see yourself in the new clothing before you make the decision to purchase. You assess how it fits, what you look like wearing it, and how you feel wearing it. You might even imagine yourself wearing it at the specific event you are purchasing it for or create in your mind an event that it would be perfect for. You gain a vision for and a feeling about the outfit before making the decision to purchase it. You might also do this when staring at your wardrobe before an important meeting, pulling out several outfits, suits, ties, shoes, and belts, trying each on, looking at yourself in the mirror, and perhaps asking someone for their opinion. The goal is to assess how you feel in the outfit and if it is the feeling you want and the image you hope to portray at the meeting. Creating a vision is very much like the process of trying on an outfit.

Goals and Vision

A goal is best defined as the object of a person's ambition or effort. It is often presented as a tangible objective, intention, plan, or purpose. For example, Neil's goal was to become a regional sales director for his company within the next two years.

A vision is the actual experience of seeing something in a dream or in your mind, almost in a supernatural manner. For example, Neil had a vision of someday being a regional sales director with his company. He could see his exact office and his team, and could see himself addressing them in the annual sales meeting. He could feel his pride in being a leader of this great team.

A goal is an intentional objective, while vision is a visual experience, seen and felt within you. It is common in business to enter the quarter or year with defined goals and objectives. But what about vision? While a goal is a target to focus intentional actions towards achieving, it is vision that adds passion, commitment, and power to reaching the goal. It is vision that clarifies feelings, values, and long-term desires.

Prior to founding my company, I knew my goal was to work with and develop leaders in business. But I wasn't certain I knew the specifics of what that looked like. Similar to the approaches I shared with Sofia, I reviewed different leadership-oriented companies and spoke with colleagues to better understand their work, companies, and job details. With every interaction I found myself "trying it on." I imagined myself working with them or in similar companies. I imagined the results of the work, the clients and people I would be working with, the logistics of each day and week, the office setting, the work-related travel, the opportunities to impact others and make a difference, and the impact the job would have on my family, my time, and my schedule. The entire process was incredibly exciting because I was creating a vision as I tried on these roles – work I could see and feel and experience. I also spent time reflecting on the next five years and identifying what I honestly wanted for my life in the future, taking into consideration my core values and all that was important to me.

Then one morning during my daily quiet time, my vision became crystal clear and my goal of working with leaders was transformed into founding my own company, Focal Pointe. That moment was so powerful – the vision so clear – that the necessary action steps to achieve the goal seemed dull in comparison to the passion, feeling, and power I felt around living my vision.

What about you? Where do you see yourself in one year? Where would you like to be? What will you like to have achieved? To make those ideas and goals a vision, practice making them real by imagining the year as if it has already occurred.

Reflection Exercise 8

Fast-forward one year. Describe what you are doing and all you have achieved.

Download the Journal at: www.leadershipbychoice.com

A Shared Vision Fosters Teamwork, Resilience, and Passion

On a personal level, your vision, when truly defined, keeps you laser-focused and provides you with greater strength for overcoming obstacles along the way. In your organization, a clearly depicted vision provides everyone with clarity and direction that they can connect with and embrace at a higher strategic level. A vision ultimately brings a team or organization together. It is a common view that when delivered well connects the team at a deeper physical and emotional level than a goal or single objective.

I remember working with Ethicon, Inc. in the early days of transition from conventional "open" surgery to a less invasive approach known as *laparoscopy*. The day-to-day job of trying to change a surgeon's approach from taking a gallbladder out via a single incision of four or five inches to placing four straw-like punctures into the abdomen with trocars was incredibly challenging. Physicians had been performing open surgery for years, and the new approach, transitioning from directly touching and seeing the gallbladder to viewing it on a two-dimensional television screen or monitor, did not make sense to many of them at the time. They were quite resistant to changing the way they did surgery and buying new equipment, making my days long and difficult at times. The goal was to sell products to support the new surgical procedure, but the vision was so much larger.

Being dedicated to the company mission of "Improving the quality of life for the surgical patient" provided me with a vision of a patient waking up from surgery and feeling able to function as a result of the less invasive surgical approach. I could see the patient returning home and back to work quickly, resuming normal activity sooner. Having this greater vision and an appreciation of how my work played a part in it, I was able to gather strength, focus, and resilience during the many – and I mean *many* – challenges and push-backs from the majority of surgeons at the time. Not only did they resist the idea of this type of surgery, but they often looked at me like I was completely nuts for even working for a company with such ideas. Nonetheless, I passionately embraced the honor of being part of making this vision a reality, aligned with a greater vision that I believed would truly help and change the world of surgery and the lives of patients.

Now, some twenty-plus years later, most abdominal

surgeries are not only performed using trocars and a laparoscopic approach, but surgeons and patients have access to even more technologically advanced options for comprehensive treatment and faster recovery! **It all started with a vision and leaders who were able to share the vision in a way that others could embrace, and in so doing make the vision a reality.**

Visionaries

Medicine is not the only field for visionaries. They are all around us, historically and in our present day. Consider the way our world is today based on the vision and leadership of some of the following:

- **Milton Hershey** – Famous for developing the Hershey chocolate bar in 1900, Milton Hershey was a visionary and humanitarian. In addition to producing affordable luxury caramels and chocolates in the late 1800s, Hershey believed in providing a comfortable community for his workers, building one complete with housing, churches, parks, theaters, transportation, and eventually a boarding school for orphan boys. His vision and passion for giving back to his community continues to thrive in Hershey, Pennsylvania, today through foundations and trusts that impact education, medicine, culture, sports, and entertainment and continue to support the communities he proudly established decades ago.

- **The Wright brothers** – These two American aviators, engineers, and inventors had a vision to invent and build the first successful airplane. Their passion and ability to create a vision for others to embrace and partner alongside them resulted in success. In Simon Sinek's book *Why Start With Why?*, he shared that their success over others on the same quest resulted from starting with "why." I would add that along with knowing why, they created a vivid picture of success for their entire team to physically embrace, resulting in their collective efforts to achieve their goal, flying the first power-controlled airplane in 1903.

- **Henry Ford** – Ford had a greater vision for automobiles and transportation for America. He wanted to produce an automobile that was affordable for middle-class Americans and not just an exclusive group of the highest financial class. Although Ford did not invent the automobile or the assembly line, he used both to develop the Model T in 1908, ultimately converting an exclusive product into an affordable means of transportation and changing the world in the twentieth century.

- **Branch Rickey** – General manager of the Dodgers in 1942, Rickey had a vision to revolutionize baseball by breaking the color barrier. Through his persistence, combined with his opposition to racism, Rickey signed Jackie Robinson in 1945, the first African-American ball player, changing the face of professional baseball and helping support the civil rights movement.

- **Walt Disney** – "It started," Disney said, "with me taking my two kids around to zoos and parks. While they were on the merry-go-round riding forty times or something, I'd be sitting there trying to figure out what you could do that would be more imaginative. I got the idea for a three-dimensional thing that people could actually come and visit. I felt that there should be something built where the parents and the children could have fun together." And so the idea of theme parks with diverse attractions for the entire family was born, and he opened the first Disneyland in 1955.

- **Martin Luther King Jr.** – King was committed to a vision of equality for all across the races. He shared it and created such a vivid picture of what he saw that he was able to lead others to confidently embrace and align to this vision. He inspired many to follow in his path, to become part of the civil rights movement in the late 1950s and 1960s, and to change the world's view of race, ultimately being killed in the process. King's vision and dream continues to live well beyond his physical years on earth.

- **Mary Kay Ash** – Founder of Mary Kay Cosmetics in 1963, Ash had a vision of creating a dream company designed specifically for women, one that would reward and recognize the hard work and values of women long before flexible work schedules existed. Creating a culture focused on the freedom to prioritize God, family, and career, in that order, Ash designed a business that allowed women to work flexible hours, with unlimited earning, without compromising their commitment to their faiths and families.

- **Eunice Kennedy Shriver** – Shriver had a vision to change the way the world treated and ignored mental retardation. In her quest throughout the 1950s and 1960s she quickly noticed that there wasn't a place for children with intellectual disabilities to play. Starting in her own backyard, Shriver held summer camps for such children. Through her passion, commitment, and support of many others, including her brother and president, John F. Kennedy, legislation supporting those with intellectual disabilities was born. Continuing her summer games more formally, in 1968 the first Special Olympic Games were held in Chicago. These games currently support and recognize more than 5.6 million athletes across the world.

- **Frederick W. Smith** – The founder of Federal Express, now FedEx, had a vision for "a system specifically designed to accommodate time-sensitive shipments such as medicine, computer parts, and electronics," first presented in a college paper while he was at Yale in 1965. Despite receiving just an average grade on the paper, six years later his original vision continued to intrigue him. While owning and operating Arkansas Aviation Sales, he saw firsthand how difficult it was to get essential packages and shipments delivered within one or two days. With his college paper in mind, Smith set out to make a change, and FedEx was born in 1973, a company that has impacted and set the standard for timely and efficient delivery systems.

- **Make-A-Wish** – This foundation was begun when a group of working-class Arizona Department of Safety officers, friends, and family decided to take a single life-changing experience and broaden it to a greater vision to grant a wish for every child suffering a life-threatening medical condition. Co-founders Frank Shankwitz, Linda Bergendahl, Scott Sahl, and Tommy Austin, along with many others, were all pivotal in making a wish a reality for Chris Greicius, a seven-year-old with leukemia, in 1980. Starting with a conversation between US Customs Agent Tommy Austin and Arizona Department of Public Safety Officer Ron Cox during a nighttime stakeout, a sequence of events ensued that resulted in the Make-A-Wish Foundation three short years later in 1983. To date the foundation has made wishes come true for over 285,000 children between the ages of two and eighteen.

- **Oprah Winfrey** – "I am guided by the vision of what I believe this show can be," Oprah said in the mission statement. "Originally our goal was to uplift, enlighten, encourage and entertain through the medium of television. Now, our mission statement for *The Oprah Winfrey Show* is to use television to transform people's lives, to make viewers see themselves differently and to bring happiness and a sense of fulfillment into every home." In shepherding one of the longest running daytime talk shows (1986 – 2011), Oprah's vision was to reach and touch lives directly through television. She achieved this, and more, all starting with a vision.

Each of these people had a vision of something greater in the future. They could "see" it, feel it, and believed it was possible. And they worked towards their vision – the picture of something they felt deeply passionate about creating and achieving. If you read further about them, you will find that each was met with countless obstacles along the way. They succeeded because they held on to the vision, shared their vision, persevered, and made it happen. The Wright brothers were not alone in the development of the airplane in the early 1900s, but their vision was clearer than those of others, fueling their passion and their "why," and allowing them to be successful ahead of those working to achieve the same outcome.

Mary Kay Ash could secure a loan from the bank only through her young son because banks wouldn't loan money to women in the early 1960s. She was laughed at for believing she could run a successful business designed for women following the priorities she outlined.

But these people didn't achieve their visions alone. It was sharing their vision with others, painting a picture of their dream for others to embrace, that yielded the collaboration and teamwork needed to be successful. Only with the belief and support of others who were inspired to work with them were these visionaries able to see their visions through to completion.

Reflection Exercise 9

How might sharing the vision you created in Exercise 8
contribute to your ability
to make it a reality?
Describe a time in your current work when you
experienced the benefits (or challenges) of being aligned
(or not aligned) to a common vision.

Download the Journal at: www.leadershipbychoice.com

Your Turn

What these people created resulted in corporations, systems, products, and services that have significantly changed and impacted the very world we live in. They created communities, jobs, awareness, and opportunities. *Your vision can do the same.* Each of them worked with just the right people, or experienced a sequence of events that influenced and impacted them, ultimately allowing them to create and manifest their vision. I would argue that everyone involved in their journeys played a significant role in the evolution of the products and services we enjoy today, including their parents, families, teachers, educators, supervisors, colleagues, spiritual leaders – the list is endless.

Regardless of what role you play, it is imminent. Right now – today – you are already making an impact. And while you might not always be able to see the complete effect of your work and interactions, you are already creating change. Regardless of your role in the creation of an idea, you could be the very fuel igniting or energizing great vision in others, today. Your contribution is as important as that of the person who receives the accolades. Without your leadership, your influence, and your ultimate impact, many future visionaries we have yet to recognize may miss their calling, their ability to maximize their gifts, and their confidence to make a difference.

Reflection Exercise 10

Who has influenced your professional journey, development, and accomplishments?
How have you played a role in helping others realize their potential?

Download the Journal at: www.leadershipbychoice.com

My Vision

It is my vision that more people will embrace their opportunity to authentically lead – to make a difference today and not wait until tomorrow, or the next job, or the next promotion. Writing *Leadership By Choice* is part of my effort to reach more of you to share my vision, my hope, my dream for you today in the workplace. And while the thought of "putting myself out there" is insanely scary, my vision and calling is so much greater that the task of writing this book, and the vulnerability of sharing my heart and possibly being criticized, are dim in comparison to the passion I have to play my part in this vision I have been given. And I mean *given*. I simply want people to love their work and their roles and to help each other be really great at their jobs! I want each of you to embrace your authentic leadership style and presence *now*. As a leader you have the greatest opportunity to influence this transformation in the workplace.

The Power of Visioning

But that is only the beginning. To make this vision real and give it life requires a bit more work. Visioning has been used for eons, and corresponds to the tenets of the Law of Attraction. The basic premise is this: We attract whatever we think about, good or bad. I have personally used it for years with a variety of big goals, the two most recent being the founding of my company on a professional level and the running of my first half-marathon on a personal level. I unequivocally feel that visioning is powerful and works! I'm not alone in this belief.

- Athletes have used it for years. It has been demonstrated repeatedly that when runners visualize running their races they can actually elevate their heart rate to their race pace simply by engaging in deep visualization.

- Hypnotists and psychotherapists use it clinically.

- Oprah Winfrey is a fan of the Law of Attraction and devoted an entire episode of her show to how it can change lives, featuring actor Jim Carrey. Carrey shared that early in his acting career he set a goal for himself using visualization. He wrote a check to himself for ten million dollars and on the memo line of that check he wrote "for acting services rendered." He kept the check tucked away in his wallet for years. Sure enough, a short ten years later he received a check for that amount "for acting services rendered."

Create a Vision

To practice creating a vision you can embrace and share with those around you, start with one of your goals. It doesn't matter the size or magnitude of the goal, but it should be one you feel strongly about. Try to add clarity to the goal by adding S.M.A.R.T. elements. First referenced in 1981 by George T. Doran, and later noted in Peter Drucker's "management by objective," the SMART acronym has taken on many variations but most commonly stands for Specific, Measureable, Achievable, Realistic, and Time-Based. Being sure your goal meets each of these criteria ensures that it is achievable.

Once your goal is clear, you can start to build a visual image of what accomplishing the goal looks like and feels like. Try it on. Imagine yourself in the moment you have achieved the goal and capture all you are thinking in that moment. Imagine the feelings you have knowing you achieved this goal, who you are sharing this accomplishment with, what you are most proud of, what it means for you now that the goal has been reached, what you conquered to get where you are, and what core values you are honoring in reaching this milestone. The visual image allows you to feel and experience the accomplishment of the goal before it has happened. Once your brain and body connect to what you "see," work on achieving your goal consciously and subconsciously until attained. This gives you a visual journey and endgame to embrace.

Reflection Exercise 11

Build visual images of successful achievements based on one professional and one personal goal.

Download the Journal at: www.leadershipbychoice.com

Visualization Is Dynamic

My gait changed as I gingerly limped on my right foot, bearing the weight and momentum with my left. I recalibrated the next twelve miles in my head, knowing that all I had visualized prior would change. I could already see my son at the finish line, waiting. I envisioned seeing him and the joy I would feel knowing we both achieved this. I could already hear the dialogue I would be having with him and my family later that day. I could hear myself telling the story of how the pain subsided and I was able to finish… and then it did.

You would think that at that point I might be telling myself what an idiot I was being, and somewhat crazy – but I was not. I had such a crystal-clear vision of crossing the finish line that for me to stop at one mile would've been far worse than doing what I did to achieve that goal that was so vivid in my brain. And it's not that I was foolishly obsessed with the goal or receiving a medal, but I couldn't release the feeling I imagined crossing the finish line. I think deep down I had already lived encompassing the goal, and saw no option other than to finish the race. I had seen it all for weeks – the entire journey. So despite a change in a part of the journey, I was able to quickly create a modified vision, still connecting with the feelings, the values of achievement, and overcoming adversity, which hadn't changed, and in fact had become even stronger, and in the end never missed a step, literally. That is the power of visualization.

True visualization is about embodying the journey as well as the accomplishment. Because part of your vision includes the journey, you can deviate from your plan without feeling derailed. The journey is about seeing, feeling, experiencing, and believing – truly believing your vision will happen. You can adjust your journey instantaneously as needed. As you master the practice of visioning you will experience the power and ability to use it in many aspects of your life.

I share this experience to underline how visualization has helped me in my journey. I want the same for you. I want you to understand how critical and impactful truly visualizing the outcome of what you seek is and how it will help you get there.

Visualization and Leadership

The visionary leaders noted earlier in the chapter produced tangible results such as a product or service – the first affordable automobile, expedited freight service, eradicating the race barrier in baseball, serving children with intellectual disabilities and those faced with life-threatening medical diagnoses. What about a vision of leadership? How can you visualize something that's not tangible?

When you think of the type of leader you aspire to be, what comes to your mind? Reflect on your core values and see how they fit into your image of you as a leader. Visualize yourself in the following scenarios to prepare to be the leader you would like to be in each one. Try it on and see what you discover.

- Negotiating with a high-potential client
- Networking with key decision-makers
- Conducting client presentations
- Handling a challenging confrontation
- Interacting with a challenging colleague
- Conducting a team meeting
- Participating in a team meeting
- Reviewing team goals for the year, quarter, and month
- Reviewing your goals with your supervisor for the year, quarter, and month
- Sitting among colleagues as part of the leadership team in your company
- Conducting a performance review with a star employee
- Conducting a performance review with a struggling employee
- Participating in your own performance review
- Working with your team to overcome an obstacle
- Interviewing job candidates

- Getting a promotion you have been working towards

- Receiving the announcement about your promotion

- Delivering "bad" news to your team

- Rewarding your team for a job well done

- Promoting one of your team members

- Addressing your team with their families present

If none of these scenarios fit your situation, create your own that make sense. Anticipate possible scenarios you might be faced with in the future, or create imaginary ones, taking the time to really "see" how you wish to lead. Explore the values you hope to honor and keep in the forefront of your visualized depiction. Practice seeing the scenarios, framing them as if they have already happened and you are reflecting on how they went. Truly start to see what you are working to create.

Reflection Exercise 12

What type of leader do you aspire to be?

Download the Journal at: www.leadershipbychoice.com

Keep Your Vision in Sight

Once you have started the process of visioning, you might find it helpful to create reminders to keep your vision alive in your head and heart. There are several ways to do this. I randomly place words or symbols around my work space to remind me of the vision I am embracing. For example, while writing this book I printed a page with the title and handwritten notes from my closest friends and colleagues congratulating me on completing the book. It might seem corny, but it reinforced my commitment to completing the book and kept me in a positive frame of mind from the very beginning. When I ran the half-marathon, there was a vision in my mind that played out in every training run – I could see and feel myself crossing the finish line and feeling on top of the world as I personally conquered a goal I had thought unattainable. In my business, I could see my clients, I could envision my work, and I could feel the humility and honor of partnering with exceptional people to make a lasting difference. A close friend and colleague of mine uses vision boards – physical depictions of the future with the goal having been achieved.

Rose sat with her sales team. It was January of 2017. The team consisted of eight members, six of whom were brand new, and the other two had been with the company for years. She was a highly determined and driven type-A achiever with the task of motivating her team to believe that they could achieve Division of the Year.

Yet there was no precedent. They had not worked together for long. The two seasoned members were not very open to new ideas, let alone anything "touchy-feely." In fact, neither was Rose. She didn't believe in mixing her personal life with her professional life, and the thought of sharing anything remotely personal not only didn't seem professional, but she wasn't eager to share her "other side" with them.

Her "other side" was as a single mother of four boys under the age of fourteen, working around the clock to maintain a happy, thriving household while sharing custody with her unemployed ex-husband. The responsibility of the finances completely lay in her hands. She took her work seriously, as it was her lifeline for supporting her growing and very hungry boys. She had to manage her schedule meticulously to maximize her time, and do all her travel for work when the boys were with their father so that when she had the boys for her half of the week she was able to be home in the evenings to fulfill her even larger job and role of being their mother.

Exposing this side of her life to her team might make her appear vulnerable, weak, and less of a leader. In Rose's world, she couldn't risk losing her credibility as a strong, bold, and determined leader in a fast-paced, growing company. Until now.

While her passion for her family danced in her head, she took a deep breath and kicked off the meeting. Being a highly accomplished, driven woman, she decided it was time for a change. Through some reflection and coaching she had realized that she had the gift of leading herself to achieve much. But she hadn't shared this gift with those around her. Today it was time, for better or worse, to share one of her secrets with her team: the power of visualization.

She stood in front of her team prepared to expose herself in ways she never had in her prior five years as a manager. She was going to show them her vision board. And in so doing, she was going to teach them how to make one for themselves. At face value the idea might seem benign, however her vision board represented both her professional and personal goals. Since her goals were dependent on her teams' productivity, she felt it was time to share all of it.

By the end of Rose's presentation her team clearly saw her vision for herself and them. They saw pictures of "Division of the Year"; of commission checks of five figures; of triathlon medals; of women crossing finish lines of marathons. They saw Rose's children laughing and happy, an elaborate vacation at Wrightsville Beach, people in love, and coffee and wine and cheese boards. They saw a baby grand piano and appreciation for music. They saw images of love, joy, peace, and bliss. They felt accomplishment, determination, and milestones. They felt the value of financial compensation and the role it played for her children. They saw the life she envisioned for herself and her future goals and accomplishments as if she'd already achieved them.

For the two who had worked with her for some time, some of the poster was not surprising – the work goals, the sales numbers, the commission checks, the drive, the determination, the hard work. However, the other parts – the family; the boys; her as a single mother, a competitive athlete, and a sole provider – they had not been exposed to.

When she concluded her presentation she handed them each a neatly rolled piece of white poster paper. It was then they realized they would be next – to dream, visualize, claim their goals – and yes, share on a deep level what they aspired to and dreamed about, not just regarding their jobs but how those very jobs supported and integrated with the other sides of their lives.

For some, sharing this with their peers was a common practice; but not for all. Watching their very strong and somewhat stoic boss expose her values, her heart, her core, was a great first step towards doing the same. So the exercise of visualizing the next year began for this young sales team, a task none of them had ever done together.

One year later, the results are in. This proud sales team achieved second place in their company and three of the eight team members finished the year in the top 10 percent. If you were to speak to those three individually, each of them would attribute their success to having a crystal-clear vision of their annual goals – a vision they reflected on daily, evidenced on their vision boards, constantly embedding in them a feeling of achievement and personal joy in reaching their goals. They eagerly waited for their annual holiday gifts to arrive: neatly scrolled pieces of white poster paper with new sets of markers. They knew what to do, and couldn't wait to prepare for their kick-off meeting of the new year in which they would get to share with their team their vision for the new year.

When you can see your vision, feel it, and experience it, regardless of the journey you take you will know when you get there. When you share your vision with others, creating a clear picture of the destination, you actively inspire others to do the same and join you on the journey.

Reflection Exercise 13

APPLICATION: Create a visual aid to keep your vision clearly in front of you.

Download the Journal at: www.leadershipbychoice.com

CHAPTER 3

Master Your Energy

Energy: the strength and vitality required for sustained physical or mental activity.

Physical Energy

There I was, running between Gates A and C in the Atlanta airport with minutes to catch the last flight home after a long few days away. Heels in hand, never making them back onto my feet after the lengthy security line, overstuffed computer bag weighing down my shoulder, and wheelie bag trailing behind me… in a skirt. It was a lovely sight, I am certain, and all too common lately. So much for professional attire – and God forbid I forego the heels for ugly flats, or sneakers even! As I rushed to the gate, onto the plane, and settled in my seat, sweating (no, glistening!) I couldn't help but be reminded of the role physical fitness plays in my ability to do my job – or catch a plane!

I could write an entire book on the direct correlation of physical fitness and physical energy to workplace productivity, as many already have. Let's face it; regardless of your profession or role, you need physical endurance and stamina to work! Leading executives know this and incorporate fitness and strength-training into their lives. If you don't believe me, next time you are on a business trip head down to the hotel exercise room at 5:00am. You will hear pounding on the treadmills being propelled by highly driven and successful professionals determined to get a workout in before the rest of the world awakens. Most are focused, quietly engaged in their own space, headsets on and most likely multitasking by getting their daily meditation and inspiration, listening to TED talks or other favorite podcasts, or catching up on news. Some are quietly focused without any input other than the sound of their soles connecting with the leather belt moving swiftly on the treadmill below them, the beating of their hearts pushing nourishing, oxygen-rich blood to their brains for clarity, to their muscles for strength, and to their core for stability. For those in this room, one of the keys of their success and their ability to maximize their endurance and stamina to do their jobs to their best potential is starting each day with some form of exercise.

Your physical well-being is easy to take for granted until you don't have it, no matter how minor the infraction. Think of a time you stubbed your baby toe. Yes, that little digit that sits on the outside of your foot, seemingly useless until you break it or stub it. It is then that you realize how much you depend on it for balance and need to have it fit into your shoe properly – the shoe that is your primary mode of transportation and which you also take for granted – the toe that goes unnoticed every day until that day when every step screams, reminding you of its very loud and important presence!

Or think of having a "small" head cold or headache. Your ability to think and function at optimum productivity is altered. Reading your smart phone, answering emails, speaking with colleagues, addressing clients – it is all impacted. Even with some of the greatest medications, your mental capacity is directly encumbered by your reduced well-being, and therefore your ability to do your best job at work, or in some cases even show up at work, is hampered. This is true for those around you as well, which is why corporate wellness has made its way into many companies' mission statements and annual budgets. **Businesses recognize that healthy, fit employees are more productive and more capable of doing their jobs well.**

You, too, already know this. With every client, friend, and colleague, the conversation about physical fitness, or the desire to be more active, comes up. And "I need to get back to the gym," "I need to get running again," or something similar, is always followed by "I feel so great when I am more active. I can't figure out why it is so hard to put exercise back into my schedule?"

Something Is Better than Nothing

While you cannot control all the physical and health challenges that may come your way, you can work towards fueling your physical energy, fitness, and well-being to hopefully control that which you can. When was the last time you evaluated your choices regarding physical fitness? Do yourself a favor and do *not* fall into the all-too-common trap of "all or nothing" – you know, the January 1st "This year I will exercise daily, eat right, and sleep more" syndrome. Rather, adopt a "one level up" or "every little bit counts" approach. It is in the small, everyday decisions about how to use your time that you can contribute to your physical energy. I know you already know what this looks like for you. Choose one small change you can make right now to contribute to your short-term and long-term physical strength, energy, and well-being.

Below are some simple ideas. Choose one or two to add to your list – no major changes in your schedule, just an increased awareness of choosing movement and hydration when you can.

- Get up fifteen minutes earlier each day and stretch, really stretch! Extend your arms high above your head and reach high towards the sky; slowly bend over and touch your knees, ankles, toes, and the floor if you can. Rotate your head and neck in slow and steady circular motions, feeling the stretch in your neck and shoulders. These small but simple movements help get the blood flowing throughout your body. Take a moment now to try it!

- Add a core exercise such as a plank for thirty seconds while watching television, and gradually increase your time. A plank is a core-strengthening exercise in which you hold your body horizontally over the floor in a position similar to the up part of a push-up; then you bend your elbows 90° and rest your weight on your forearms. Your elbows should be directly beneath your shoulders, and your body should form a straight line from your head to your feet. You can choose to rest your hands flat on the floor with your palms down or clasp your hands together. Hold the position for as long as you can. This isometric exercise improves core strength including the abdominal, hamstring, and gluteal muscles ("glutes"), to name a few. If you want to feel all the muscles a plank engages, hold the position for as long as you can – you will quickly identify each muscle that contributes to a successful plank and appreciate how a single exercise can be an efficient way to impact multiple muscles simultaneously!

• Add one sixteen-ounce water bottle to your daily water intake. Studies vary on the amount of daily water intake that was shown to be optimal, but between ten and fifteen cups are recommended, depending on your gender, food consumption, activity level, and age. Each person is unique and has different needs. I found that drinking sixteen-ounce bottles of water is more palatable than other options for some reason, and strive to drink one bottle as soon as I wake up and one bottle immediately before I go to sleep, and strive to consume three more throughout my day, usually with a meal, which has proven manageable for a non-water-loving, typically under-hydrated person. If you are not particularly fond of water, try starting with one extra bottle a day, or add a little flavor to your water, such as a bit of lemon or orange juice.

- Using your phone app that already tracks your steps each day, monitor it more closely and work to increase it by 10 percent. Whether you choose to track your steps or your time of physical activity, focus on increasing increments. The American Heart Association recommends 175 minutes per week of moderate exercise, or on average thirty minutes per day, five days per week.

For those of you who are already pretty committed to fitness and want to expand your diversity, or for those who don't like exercising for exercising's sake and work better with goals, as I do:

- Schedule yourself for an event that will stretch your physical training and commitment to a higher level: register for a 5K, 10K, half-marathon, or full marathon.

- Consider a multidimensional challenge like a sprint triathlon, Spartan, or Tough Mudder.

- Try out a completely new sport: swimming, rock wall climbing, single scull or crew rowing, kayaking, paddle boarding, CrossFit®, judo, boxing, dancing, yoga, cycling, horseback riding, skiing, snowshoeing, skating… find something you have always considered doing but never took the time for.

- If increasing relationships and connections is one of your core values, consider combining fitness and building relationships by joining a sports team or training program or by adding a workout partner to your routine.

Fitness is not about *what* you choose to do but rather that you recognize that only *you* can fuel your physical energy, and as a result *choose* to engage in activities and actions that reflect that. You don't have to run a marathon; just move a level up from your current level of activity. By choosing to increase your fitness and stamina, you will directly increase your ability to be more present with your colleagues and have greater all-around impact. With increased physical energy, your concentration, decision-making, and overall presence will improve, helping you be more efficient and productive.

Reflection Exercise 14

What is one strategy you can choose to improve your physical energy and overall well-being today?

Download the Journal at: www.leadershipbychoice.com

Attitudinal Energy

As the words rolled off my manager's tongue and into my ears I felt an explosion in my brain. The burst quickly communicated an internal "No way!" causing my adrenaline and cortisol to rise and subsequent nausea deep inside, traveling down my throat and landing in my gut. "Stay calm," I thought, "and focus – after all, you just finished training the new sales team in the next room… this makes no rational sense." The sound of her voice became muffled as I watched her lips continue to move, imparting a controlled and scripted message. The words, although confusing and contradictory, were delivering a crystal-clear message: I was no longer going to be able to keep my job as I knew it and needed to consider different options, demotions… and they needed a decision immediately.

When I sat in my manager's office that day I was at the height of experiencing conflict, stress, and negative energy. I would later learn to call it *catabolic energy*. I had to make a choice, and while the choice appeared to be what I wanted to do about my job, the real choice – the deeper choice – was realized months later. The choice was not about the job but about how to choose to *be* as a result of this experience. Did I want to live feeling angry, bitter, resentful, like a victim, and like the circumstances were outside of my control? And if so, for how long? Or would I rather focus on the silver lining and invest my energy in creating something great out of something that felt pretty darn awful? Did I want to be strong and focused on what was in front of me, put the past behind me, and move on? Could I choose to be positive about the experience and find the opportunity in it, accessing my typically positive attitude?

This one was tough, probably one of the most challenging times in my life. Nonetheless I had a choice in this and it was time to choose my attitude. I chose to be positive and was quickly reminded of the power of positive thinking. It was not the first time I had been reminded of this, and quickly I remembered that not only did it feel better, but having the ability to maintain a positive attitude could contribute to a competitive advantage as well. I had witnessed it not only in myself over the years but in my sales team years prior:

I watched the reactions of my sales team of ten after I had shared with them the adjusted compensation plan for the upcoming year. Without missing a beat,

- *One person immediately got quiet, almost withdrawn, and I questioned if he was even listening to the complete message. It was an unsettling acceptance of the plan – not a positive or negative response, simply a "whatever" type of response that made me wonder what he was thinking.*

- *Three people quickly calculated (and abruptly verbalized) their net loss based on the new plan versus the current plan, and were unhappy and openly angry about it. They were my fighters – quick to express their frustration whenever they heard news that might be perceived as wrong or unfair.*

- *Simultaneously I observed three others diligently working the new plan and trying to overlay a refined strategy to maximize their commissions. These were my engine – the ones who always managed to find a way to get things done despite how they initially felt, rationalized a brighter outlook, and could quickly step into action and find a way to achieve the goals in front of them.*

- *One member of my team looked over at me, concerned by the negativity of the vocal group, and smiled, offering a silent message of compassion and understanding, always concerned about the overall team cohesiveness above herself.*

- *Another openly strategized with the team regarding ways they might be able to better work together, leveraging each of their areas of expertise to create an overall win for the team with the new compensation plan. He constantly worked to encourage the team to look ahead, not get bogged down in the details, and work together to find strength and opportunities to succeed.*

- *The last member of my team genuinely never seemed phased by compensation, good or bad. For the most part, little ever rattled him. He exuded a sense of calm, and faith in the system per se, and aired a sense that everything always works out as it should. Sometimes my more expressive representatives couldn't relate to his sense of calm, especially during critical month-end runs to achieve forecast when emotions were high. Nonetheless he offered an unshakeable sense of peace that mostly served the team well.*

Those who were able to move into a strategy to maximize the new compensation plan were able to quickly create a viable game plan for themselves. Those who were consumed by how this change would negatively affect them took longer. In the following weeks while they were stuck feeling frustrated and complaining, both internally and outwardly, focusing on what would have or could have been, the others had long since moved on and were well into making sales and earning commissions in the leading categories, choosing to maximize their situation and meet company forecasts. They clearly had an advantage because regardless of their initial feelings about the changed compensation plan, they chose to move beyond the negativity quickly, found a way to create a win, and moved into action, swiftly embracing the adjusted course.

It was vividly clear to me at that time how attitude directly impacted performance and outcomes. That one situation evoked ten very different responses – some downright negative and helpless; others more positive with varying degrees of engagement, commitment, strategizing, and forward action. Maybe you have experienced a similar situation.

Your Turn

Think of situations in which you received less than favorable news that required you to adjust your thinking or approach. Do you tend to linger in frustration or anger, sharing your thoughts with multiple friends and colleagues about the negative situation; or are you able to quickly shift from your initial negative feelings towards more positive ones? How would you describe your overall attitude? Positive? Negative? Optimistic? Pessimistic? Another description? How would your close friends and colleagues describe your attitude?

You might have heard some of these quotes about attitude:

- "When life gives you lemons, make lemonade!" (author unknown)

- "Your attitude, not your aptitude, will determine your altitude." – Zig Ziglar

- "Life is 10% what happens to me and 90% how I react to it. And so it is with you." – Charles R. Swindoll

...the corresponding interpretations being:

- When something bad comes your way, use it to make something good.

- Your attitude contributes more to your ability to achieve than your intellect does.

- How you react to the events in your life is more important than the events themselves.

It appears to be fairly straightforward: Regardless of the situation or event, your response is either more positive than negative, or more optimistic than pessimistic. While "positive" tends to feel better, and is often more acceptable in the workplace, at times "negative" feels necessary, earned, and gratifying to express! Take a moment to reflect on a time when you were able to maintain a positive attitude while others could not. How did your attitude in this situation help you? What about a reverse situation in which others around you were generally optimistic about something and you struggled to share their optimism?

Reflection Exercise 15

How would you describe your overall attitude?

Download the Journal at: www.leadershipbychoice.com

At that moment in my manager's office that I shared with you above, and in the following months, my head wanted to be positive. It was who I tried to be. But I didn't feel that in my heart. I was angry and hurt. What I really felt was:

- Sour, like I was in a blender being emulsified

- Like my "Susie Sunshine" positive attitude had gotten me nowhere

- Like I was losing professional altitude and would crash hard

- Stuck in the reality of life just happening, reacting negatively, and having little to no ability to change its course or see anything beyond my current situation; in other words, a victim of my circumstances

I was stuck and unclear about the future. While I knew I needed to shift my attitude, it was not as easy as I thought it would be. I needed guidance and understanding. In my head the choice was clear. However, to get my heart to follow my head I had to dig deep and go to one of my innermost core values and guiding philosophies to find resolve – one that undeniably comforts me when I feel lost:

Trust in the Lord with all your heart and lean not on your own understanding, but in all ways acknowledge Him and He will direct your paths.
– Proverbs 3:5–6

And I remembered something my mother always said to me in difficult times: "When one door closes, another one always opens."

I certainly had no understanding other than that I needed to have faith, look at the path in front of me, choose my next door, and work to make something good out of this. I needed to create opportunity. It was time to throw the sour lemons in the blender, add a lot of *real* sugar (nothing fake) and water, and MAKE SOME SERIOUS LEMONADE! I chose to honor my core values, and yes, trust in God to direct my path. At that moment I intentionally shifted my thoughts, which directly impacted my ability to see opportunities and find the good in the situation. By making a conscious decision to shift my energy and focus, I was able to transition from feeling stuck to feeling empowered to move forward. I shifted my attitude; and I believe that same choice exists for you as well. What do you do when you are feeling stuck? When your head and heart are at odds? Who or what do you turn to for support and guidance?

Reflection Exercise 16

Who or what do you turn to when feeling stuck or needing guidance?

Download the Journal at: www.leadershipbychoice.com

Thoughts, Feelings, Actions – It's Physical

Numerous studies have been conducted that supported a definitive correlation between our thoughts and our corresponding physiological responses. The *placebo effect* continues to be researched and studied. While placebos themselves do not cure disease, they have often been associated with a decrease in symptoms due to the patient's belief in the "medicine" they took, or in some cases an increase in side effects associated with the drug believed to have been taken. ("The Power of the Placebo Effect," Harvard Medical School, May 2017, https://www.health.harvard.edu/mental-health/the-power-of-the-placebo-effect) This diagram makes it easier to understand:

You have a thought!
    It stimulates your brain.
        Your brain sends a message in response to your thought,
        producing hormones.
           The hormones contribute to feelings.
             The feelings contribute to emotions.
               The emotions cause you to take action.
    Action fosters more thoughts.
And the cycle repeats itself.

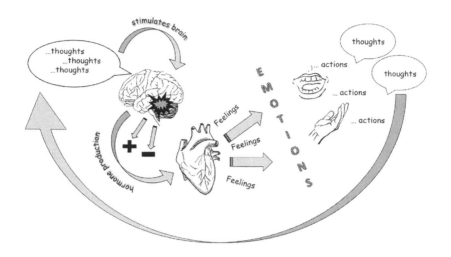

When you have a positive thought your brain sends a positive message to your body, resulting in a particular physiological chain of events; and when you have a negative thought your brain sends a negative message to your body, resulting in a different physiological chain of events. The message your brain sends prompts the production of hormones and neurotransmitters, such as cortisol, adrenaline, endorphins, serotonin, oxytocin, and dopamine, to name a few, which contribute to different physiological outcomes, actions, and subsequent thoughts.

To further demonstrate this concept, imagine that your alarm clock goes off in the morning. Immediately a thought is ignited in your brain – either "Wow, it's going to be a great day; I can't wait to get out of bed – I have so much to achieve today and I can't wait to do it!" or "Ugh, I am sooo tired and burned out. I can't do this today. Isn't it the weekend yet?! Just ten more minutes..." or possibly "ARGHHH, I'm late! I overslept!!" Based on your initial thoughts, your brain immediately sends a message in your body that result in a sequence of events and subsequent actions. For example:

Thought	Wow, it's going to be a great day – I have so much to achieve today and can't wait!	Ugh, I am sooo tired and burned out…I can't do this today.	ARGHHH, I'm late!
Category	Positive	Negative	Negative with imminent stress
Possible hormones	Serotonin and Dopamine	Cortisol	Adrenaline and Cortisol
Feelings	Peace and joy	Lethargy and stress	Anxiety and stress
Action	Rise out of bed with a sense of happy, peaceful entry into the day.	Hit the snooze and go back to sleep.	Jump out of bed, heart racing, as you run to get dressed and out the door.
Thought	I am going to get so much accomplished today!	None – you are asleep, possibly preparing for the ARGHHH thought when you realize you overslept.	I HATE when this happens! My whole day just got ruined. How did this happen… again?!

A sequence of thoughts has already started and you are just starting your day!

Thoughts and Stress

Think of a time in your life when you felt under stress. You may not even have labeled it "stress," but you felt ill at ease and had an underlying intense, conflicted feeling inside of you. I'm sure you know the feeling, and you most likely know the typical contributors for you: approaching deadlines, pressure at work, finances, unsettled disagreements, relationship challenges, not enough sleep or exercise, too many meals on the run, lacking quality time with family, too much to do and not enough time to do it, countless responsibilities, commitments.... The feeling usually results from a conglomeration of individually manageable contributors, but once piled sequentially or simultaneously they become the perfect storm, yielding varying levels of stress.

According to the Mayo Clinic, your body's natural stress response functions as follows: When you are faced with a stressful event an alarm system is set off in your brain, triggering the production of hormones including adrenaline and cortisol. These two hormones contribute to increased heart rate, blood pressure, sugar, and glucose levels in the blood, enabling the ability and thought to respond when faced with fear or stress. When the perceived threat has passed, the hormone levels return to normal, and with them heart rate, blood pressure, and other impacted bodily systems. However, in the presence of constant stress and the corresponding continual elevated levels of adrenaline, cortisol, and other stress-related hormones, the results are damaging to your entire body's systems. "This puts you at an increased risk of numerous health problems including: anxiety, depression, digestive problems, headaches, heart disease, sleep problems, weight gain, memory and concentration impairment. That's why it's so important to learn healthy ways to cope with the stressors in your life." ("Chronic Stress Puts Your Health at Risk," https://www.mayoclinic.org/healthy-lifestyle/stress-management/in-depth/stress/art-20046037)

When you hold on to thoughts and feelings that cause stress, you limit your ability to see and act on alternative options to the very things that are causing you stress. It can be a vicious cycle that you know you need to break, but it can be difficult to do so.

In some circumstances your body can even communicate your level of stress before you consciously acknowledge feeling stressed. For example, you feel soreness or pain in parts of your body, you have more frequent headaches, your appetite or your ability to sleep deviates from the norm, or you find yourself getting sick more frequently.

Learning to recognize and manage stress plays an essential part in your ability to lead yourself and others. Understanding your thoughts and their direct impact on your overall attitude is a great first step to increasing your ability to shift from thought patterns that contribute to stress.

Reflection Exercise 17

What is currently causing you stress?
How might you minimize or eliminate this stress?

Download the Journal at: www.leadershipbychoice.com

When my manager told me that I was not going to be able to keep my job as I knew it, once I decided to "make lemonade" and shifted my energy I started to feel better. I had no knowledge of the physiological boost I had created by making this choice, but the doors that subsequently opened brought me across thresholds I never could have imagined! In my coaching work I had the tremendous opportunity to study and become certified in Energy Leadership™, a model developed by Bruce D. Schneider, founder of the Institute of Professional Excellence in Coaching, who has dedicated most of his research to the impact of stress and attitude in the workplace today.

Anabolic and Catabolic Energy Defined

In his book *Energy Leadership*, Schneider described energy as the potential people have for success in their lives. He introduced two types of energy: anabolic and catabolic. Anabolic energy releases testosterone (among other hormones), and is positive, constructive, inspiring, and growth-oriented; while catabolic energy, which releases cortisol and adrenalin, is draining, limiting, destructive, and harmful. In the workplace, "Anabolic leaders have the ability to motivate and inspire themselves and others to do extraordinary things. They have the ability to make energetic shifts in all levels of the organization. Catabolic leaders break down all aspects of a company, including the people in it," according to Schneider. (Bruce D. Schneider, *Energy Leadership*, (Hoboken, NJ: Wiley, 2007))

Catabolic Energy in the Workplace

Most likely you have experienced a catabolic person in your career. It is your colleague, manager, or someone who reports to you who is constantly creating conflict, is under pressure, or creates pressure. They tend to view situations as black or white, right or wrong. Their energy can include a sense of being frustrated with work and life in general or a specific issue. This is probably someone you don't enjoy being around or can take only in small doses. They suck the life out of you and the team. Just being in their negative – or catabolic – presence is challenging. They tend to be contrary, and fighters. They can't seem to find the good in anything. Everything is a battle, a challenge – as if the negativity in the world or from the job is personally directed at them. They react as though they never get a break and are constantly fighting a losing battle. If you work for this person you might get a lot done, as there is constant pressure to achieve, but the catabolic environment becomes one you resent over time, and it can be physically stressful and ultimately detrimental to your overall well-being.

Anabolic Energy in the Workplace

Now take a moment to reflect on colleagues you have worked with who truly inspired you – perhaps a leader under whom you thrived or a colleague you felt invigorated to work around. Most likely they demonstrated anabolic energy and were generally positive and upbeat about work and their role. They exuded confidence and a sense of peace and optimism regarding the business, regardless of the challenges. You felt inspired, confident, and capable in the presence of this leader. They had an ability to find opportunity in everything and to navigate conflicts and obstacles with relative ease, almost as if embracing them. They were visionary and not afraid to dream. Your ability to perform and realize your full potential improved just by being in their presence.

Your Choice

In summary, the person with catabolic energy repelled you and the person with anabolic energy attracted you. When you reflect on your own presence and energy, do you think you repel or attract others? When you walk into a room full of people, do you elevate the overall mood, energy, or disposition, or do you diminish it? Regardless of your answer today, you have the ability to *choose* your answer moving forward.

Similar to choosing to improve your physical energy, you can also choose to improve and build your attitudinal energy. It starts by increasing your awareness of this topic, and by simply reading this book you have initiated your awareness! How you choose to improve your energy and attitude further relates to your ability to have tremendous impact and influence moving forward.

Seven Levels of Energy

I have directly witnessed the transformation of leaders like you when they chose to shift their attitude from catabolic to anabolic. It starts with assessing and understanding your default energy, and then intentionally working to create the energy you aspire to. Working with Energy Leadership as a Certified Energy Leadership Master Practitioner, and further exploring the "7 Levels of Energy" model developed by Bruce Schneider, I am able to take clients' understanding of catabolic and anabolic energy to a much deeper level, and work with them to consciously alter their approach and attitude to maximize outcomes.

The power you can gain as you intentionally work to master your attitudinal energy is substantial. Like building your physical energy, building your adaptability and strength requires accessing resources and tools for doing so. With improved energy your ability to communicate, connect, and problem-solve also improves. Your presence becomes more positive, and you become that person who ignites passion, creativity, and inspiration in yourself and those around you, ultimately maximizing your impact and influence in the workplace, right where you are.

I like to use the basic principles of 7 Levels of Energy with my clients to help them re-create their thoughts in real-world scenarios. Each of the levels of energy affords different perspectives, attitudinal energy choices, and opportunities for varying degrees of impact, influence, and inspiration for yourself and those around you.

To identify how Schneider's 7 Levels of Energy applies to my team members' responses to the new compensation plan that I outlined earlier in the chapter, I separated them by levels as follows:

Catabolic Energy	Level 1	Victim; Helpless; No ability to impact change	One was immediately quiet and helpless. He didn't feel he could have any impact. It was what it was – "Oh well, whatever."
	Level 2	Fighter; Angry; Feeling of losing a win/lose scenario	Three were angry and stated that the compensation plan would hurt them.
Anabolic Energy	Level 3	Competitive, Rationalizer; Find a way or make a way to win	Three immediately strategized how to get the job done and maximize compensation, or win.
	Level 4	Selfless; Service; Concern for others winning above oneself	One was focused on helping maintain peace at the meeting, mostly concerned for others.
	Level 5	Team focus; See opportunity for all to win	One strategized how the team could benefit collectively from the combined strengths and group expertise.
	Level 6	Winning/losing – all the same; It is all good, always	One seemed genuinely fine with the new plan and ready to move ahead with whatever, exuding a sense of inner peace and calm.
	Level 7	Pure peace; No judgment either way	No one fit this energy.

You might already have access to some of the tools or references from prior experience with Schneider's model. If you have had the opportunity to experience Energy Leadership, go back to your training materials and take time to review them. If not, here are several options to consider in mastering your attitudinal energy:

- Participate in an Energy Leadership Index Assessment and Debrief.

- Build your knowledge and awareness of Energy Leadership by visiting **www.focalpointeinc.com/ leadership-services/**

- Consider participating in a 360-degree Energy Leadership Assessment or a similar assessment to gain perspective on how others view your leadership attitude.

- Consider working with a certified Energy Leadership coach to help you complete a self-assessment and intention plan.

Energy Leadership is one method you can use to gain greater perspective on your overall attitude in normal situations as well as when under stress. When you put this into practice, like many of my clients you gain the ability to consciously choose and manage your attitude to maximize performance, impact, and influence. **To be an inspirational leader and make a difference, choose to create an attitude and develop energy that attracts people and opens up the world of opportunity.**

Attitude Check Alternatives

As an alternative to the Energy Leadership model, take time to honestly evaluate your overall attitude:

- Reflect on a variety of scenarios and interactions with people at work, making note of your general responses and reactions. Do you find that you have a natural tendency to make the best of challenges and to see the bright side of conflicts; or do you find yourself feeling frustrated or in conflict frequently? You might not show frustration outwardly, but if you are feeling it internally you are creating the same stress response that you are when you display your feelings openly.

- After assessing yourself as above, consider getting additional feedback. Identify one or two trusted colleagues, friends, or relatives and have honest conversations with them about what they observe about your current attitude and energy. It is always helpful to gain clarity about your own perception versus the perceptions of others.

- If this direct approach is a bit too close for comfort, consider exploring a formal "360-degree" feedback evaluation. This is a process in which an independent facilitator gathers anonymous feedback from several peers, colleagues, supervisors, and subordinates regarding your performance in specified areas. Combined with your own self-assessment, a 360 allows you to see how those closest to you view your attitude, leadership, and performance as outlined in the specific evaluative tool. Many companies offer this resource for their employees, especially those in leadership roles. Reach out to info@focalpointeinc.com for additional customized resources and evaluation tools.

- Identify one of your leaders who greatly inspired you and ask them for a tip or recommendation regarding their philosophy about leadership. Ask them for candid feedback on your strengths and areas in which you can improve your leadership influence.

- Read or listen to any of the recommended resources in the "References and Inspirations" section at the end of this book, as many of them address strategies to improve and maximize positive thinking and a healthy attitude.

Energy Runs Together

What I love so much about the topic of physical and attitudinal energy is that both can be improved with a choice. You have complete control over how you choose to build your strength and endurance. While it may be challenging at times to apply this choice to a myriad of circumstances, you always have a choice. Let that empower you to know that at any given moment, when you are ready for a change or ready to take your performance to the next level, you can. It is up to you to choose. Your physical exercise, fitness, and well-being are directly connected to your attitude – they feed each other, and it is up to you to make it happen.

When you choose to fuel your physical and attitudinal energy positively you maximize the strength and vitality required for impactful leadership.

Reflection Exercise 19

APPLICATION: What steps will you take today to positively fuel your physical and attitudinal energy?

Download the Journal at: www.leadershipbychoice.com

CHAPTER 4

Bench Press Your Barriers

For athletes to become stronger and build endurance they participate in a combination of exercise protocols involving strength training to build muscle and cardiovascular activities to build endurance. Strength-training routines often include focusing on different muscle groups on alternate days to facilitate the physiological process necessary to strengthen muscles. Working a muscle group with varying degrees of resistance (or weights) and repetition causes micro-tears in the muscle fibers. During the body's process of healing the micro-tears the muscle builds and the athlete becomes stronger.

Cardiovascular routines work in the same manner, combining interval or sprint training with longer aerobic training, building heart and lung efficiency to fuel the body and muscles to perform at increasingly longer and more demanding events. Athletes accept that to become stronger and build endurance to accomplish their goals often requires rigorous workouts and a commitment to embrace the temporary discomfort as a necessary part of their development. Therefore rather than avoid the workout, they choose to seize it as yet another hurdle to overcome to get them closer to their goal.

Building your strength and endurance as a leader is no different. And the hurdles, or barriers, are the very mechanisms to get you there, developing and preparing your thought processes and corresponding actions to have greater impact and influence.

In the first three chapters you have:

- Taken time to uncover your core values and further define what guides you in your decision-making process

- Created a vision for yourself, seeing where you want to be in the future and choosing what that looks and feels like

- Reflected on your physical and attitudinal energy, choosing to commit to developing them to set you up for success

However, regardless of the power of your values, vision, and energy, life happens. As you saw in the last chapter, at every crossroad you have a choice. But just because you recognize this does not imply that making choices is always easy or clear.

Reflecting again on your values, vision, and energy, what do you think is stopping you from getting where you want to go right now? What is preventing you from being the leader you aspire to be? Take some time to note your thoughts. You know the answer to this question better than anyone!

If you are feeling stuck in furthering your role as a leader, it might be something completely outside of your immediate control. For example, perhaps you want to be promoted within your company, but the corporate headquarters is in a different location and you can't relocate right now. Or you need to fill two positions on your team but company resources are limited and you can't fund those positions currently, requiring you to manage and meet milestones while understaffed. Or maybe you currently lead a small team, or even no one, and desperately desire to have a large team to lead, yet the position does not exist in your current work environment. While the problem may be outside of your control, your attitude and energy about it *is* in your control.

To maximize your impact and influence, choose to embrace all that slows you down and find strategies to overcome your barriers, recognizing that in this choice you are building your strength and endurance like the athlete. Learn to acknowledge and evaluate roadblocks effectively and have tools in place to work through them as efficiently as possible.

Reflection Exercise 20

What is preventing you today from being the leader you aspire to be?

Download the Journal at: www.leadershipbychoice.com

Top Ten Barriers

Based on many experiences setting, achieving, missing, and changing goals, combined with having the honor to work with, guide, mentor, and lead individuals, added to being on teams, leading teams, and in more recent years coaching individuals and teams, I have found that barriers come from two general sources that continually feed one another: attitude and aptitude.

1. Your attitude: Your mind contains your thoughts, opinions, and beliefs, which impact your attitude and subsequent actions, fueled by your inner voice – the quiet voice inside your head – feeding you positive messages or starving your overall confidence.

2. Your aptitude: Your knowledge, or skill set, is a combination of your training, experience, and physical preparedness to accomplish a task; for example, training in medicine or surgery for doctors, planning and organizational skills for project managers, and mathematical analytics for actuaries.

The combination of attitude and aptitude contributes to your overall ability or lack of ability to move towards a goal, which requires both acknowledgment of the barrier and intentional action to move beyond it. In this chapter I focus on the top barriers to your thoughts. As discussed in chapter 3, your thoughts influence how you feel, respond, and ultimately act. I have found that decision-making, choices, and actions of leaders are influenced far more by their thoughts than by their aptitude. If you want to find ways to grow and develop as an impactful leader, explore how your thinking might be creating barriers to your development and your ability to lead.

The ten common barriers that slow leaders down in achieving their goals are:

1. Conflicting values

2. An unclear vision

3. Poor energy or attitude

4. Low confidence

5. False assumptions

6. Restricting beliefs

7. Fear of success or failure

8. A poor relationship with time

9. Lack of accountability

10. Lack of communication

These barriers can apply to both short-term and long-term goals. As you reflect on your answer to what is holding you back from being the leader you aspire to be, consider how these barriers are influencing your thoughts. Your ability to successfully lead yourself relies on your ability to vividly look in the mirror, understand what's getting in your way, and work towards mastering a skill to work around it. Not only will this help you reach your goals but it will also help you impact others around you, as you will be better equipped to identify their barriers and teach them strategies to move beyond them as well. I address each barrier in more detail below.

1. Conflicting Values

When a goal or task is in direct conflict or not aligned with your core values, you can find yourself stalled in indecision, unable to move forward. As discussed in chapter 1, when I help clients identify and align with their core values, their ability to move forward with a greater sense of peace and satisfaction improves. There is something in appreciating yourself for who you are – for being totally connected to what matters most to you – that liberates and frees you, allowing you to make decisions more quickly and confidently. Here are some examples of how conflicting values can show up at work and slow you down in making decisions and moving action forward:

- A critical client is in town for two days. You would normally accompany them to dinner to seal the deal, but this particular day is your child's thirteenth birthday, and you always try to celebrate birthdays together.

- You have a goal of taking on more responsibility, climbing the ladder, but the next role is office-based and behind the scenes, limiting your ability to be in the field working face-to-face with clients, where you excel and are typically rewarded and recognized.

- You want to move into a different function at work, requiring extensive training and travel. You value the growth opportunity, yet travel will pull you away from your family extensively, placing a hardship on your spouse.

- It is the end of the month, and while your team has achieved its sales quota, the larger region has not. You are called to lead your team in going back to clients for more sales.

- You are in the process of filling a vacant position on your team and have identified two candidates who could contribute greatly. Your vice president calls you, asking you to interview another candidate, his nephew's girlfriend, who is relocating to be with his nephew. He's not familiar with her qualifications but feels she might be a great fit on your team.

To work through a barrier involving conflicting values:

- Review the exercises in chapter 1 to connect to your core values.

- As you uncover the core values in conflict, explore whether there are ways to honor your values simultaneously or an opportunity to view the conflict differently. For example, in the choice between having dinner with a key client or a birthday dinner with your child, your initial thought might be that the choices exclude each other. Explore moving the birthday dinner earlier and going to dinner with the client afterward, or consider being completely honest with the client or your child by explaining your dilemma, openly sharing your conflicting values. Perhaps one or both of them would be more than willing to accommodate a change.

I have been in this situation many times, as the hostess and as the client. And although I enjoy having dinner with clients, I have also appreciated times when they openly shared a conflict, allowing me the opportunity to bow out as well and have a quiet evening at home with my family; and when they admitted that they could use a night to catch up on work instead of a late dinner.

• Openly explain your conflicting values when they involve others. For example, in the situation about exploring a possible job change that could present a hardship to your family, include them in your thought process. While your conflicting values might be advancing your career and being physically present to support your family, your family members might be conflicted about encouraging your career growth and advancement or relying on you more than they need to. Through open dialogue you might find that you can create a viable solution for all to embrace, allowing all of you to overcome barriers involving values you felt were getting in your way.

- Practice openly sharing your values in your communications with others as those values relate to the specific goal you are working towards. For example, in response to the vice president in the situation above in which he wanted you to interview another candidate, you can say, "I welcome the opportunity to interview another candidate. *I value keeping an open mind* and choosing the most qualified person for the job. With two highly qualified candidates currently in the mix, I will add her and evaluate her qualifications as well, and let you know how the three candidates compare." Or, in the example of leading your team to solicit more sales, you might openly share, "Team, I know we have already achieved our monthly sales quota, however the region has not. *I value being a team player* and the region could use our help with some additional sales. *I also value your integrity and the relationships you have* with your clients. Please review who you feel comfortable reaching out to for additional orders this month to help us achieve this final goal, as long as it does not compromise the long-standing relationship or needs of the client."

- Work with a coach or a trusted colleague to find opportunities to honor the values you believe are being challenged, and create pathways to move ahead.

Reflection Exercise 21

As you reflect on conflicting values, how does this barrier currently impact you?

Download the Journal at: www.leadershipbychoice.com

2. An Unclear Vision

When you lack clarity regarding the vision you or your team is working towards, it contributes to lack of purpose and direction, and not being able to connect your day-to-day work to the bigger picture. Clarity of vision allows you to overcome short-term challenges and adversity in order to achieve the greater vision. With an unclear vision you can find yourself just going through the motions, feeling unattached to your work, feeling stuck, spiraling, and underachieving. As part of a team, you can find the team consumed with busywork and not unified in a common direction, ultimately falling short of goals. This is how this might present in the workplace:

- You are part of a team working on multiple projects with conflicting timelines. The hours feel endless and your quality of life is suffering. You're not even sure how these projects fit into the big picture or what the big picture really is. You feel overworked and relatively disengaged, and both you and your team repeatedly miss deadlines.

- Your company was just acquired by another company. You thought your career path was set but now you can't see the future and how this merger/acquisition will impact your career path. You feel stuck and unsure about the future.

- Your company just shelved one of three products your team was actively selling, leaving you with the job of inspiring your team to carry on despite the loss of a revenue-generating product that was also critical to the company mission and vision. The vision and plan have completely changed, and your team is complaining and possibly seeking alternative employment. You're not sure in which direction to take your team.

- The members of your organization seem to be working hard, yet you feel everyone is out of synch, rarely working harmoniously. You notice a lot of competition between departments. In a recent team meeting with an outside consultant it became clear that no one had a sense of the vision for the organization. In fact, not one person could articulate it despite it being boldly featured on a plaque in the corporate entryway. You even question if you truly understand the direction and focus of the company since it rarely is highlighted.

To add clarity to a vision:
- Starting with you, determine if you are spiraling or stuck as a result of your personal vision being unclear or as a result of your company's vision feeling unclear. Revisit your goals and the vision you are working towards.

If the vision has changed or needs to be modified, rebuild it for yourself. Using strategies from chapter 2, look ahead and visualize having completed the goal, understanding the impact you will have. What does it look like? Find a connection to your values.

- If you are having difficulty connecting the projects and activity to the greater vision of your company, seek input and guidance from your immediate supervisor to understand the connection. In turn, communicate the connection to your team, offering them a stronger sense of clarity.

- Challenge yourself to identify whether the vision is unclear or it has legitimately changed direction. In the example above, just because a product was shelved does not mean the vision has changed. The vision might be the same but the strategy to achieve the vision has changed to meet a new set of circumstances. Restate the vision, and re-create the path to get there based on the changed dynamic.

- Appreciate and embrace that sharing a vision can truly connect and align a team in committing to a common goal. That said, each person identifies with it slightly differently, and they might benefit from creating a personal vision statement specifically for them. Encourage this along with sharing everyone's vision with the team. Start by making your personal version and connection to the overall mission clear to the group.

- Use visual reminders of why you're doing what you're doing and where you see yourself in one year. Use a vision board or journal to keep your vision clearly in front of you and minimize anything that slows you down.

Reflection Exercise 22

As you reflect on your vision, how might you refine it to better support your goals moving forward?

Download the Journal at: www.leadershipbychoice.com

3. Poor Energy or Attitude

A negative attitude – or catabolic energy – can at times fuel you to get work done, but ultimately prevents you from truly growing and seeing opportunities to move forward. It's often disguised in thoughts or language such as "this is just the way it is" or "there's never enough time in the day." A poor or negative attitude can transform minor speed bumps into mountains, slowing you down and restricting your ability to move forward. This barrier can show up in the workplace as any of these situations:

- No matter how hard you work you cannot seem to get ahead.

- Everything your supervisor asks you frustrates you.

- You have little tolerance for certain people or certain tasks.

- You find that you prefer to work alone more often than usual.

- You have become reclusive and feel unable to impact change on a particular project.

- There is one particular colleague you always seem to be in conflict with, both inwardly and outwardly.

- You are a get-it-done person, always finding a way to accomplish the task and rarely seeking help, which can preclude opportunities for delegation and assistance.

- If you want it done right, you have to do it yourself.

- Numerous things about your company and work environment irritate you – it all seems fairly dysfunctional and you doubt "they" will ever get it right.

To adjust your energy and attitude:
- Check in on your physical well-being – your diet, sleep, activity level, exercise – and be sure you're fueling yourself physically to perform optimally at work. Your ability to deal with less-than-ideal environments can be reduced significantly when there are confounding issues such as sleep deprivation, lack of nourishment, or other physical challenges. If this is a contributing factor, consider adjusting your schedule to take a bit more time for your well-being.

- Imagine how you would act if your feelings were the complete opposite of your current feelings. For example, rather than feeling behind at work, you feel completely on top of it; rather than feeling frustrated, you feel inspired; rather than feeling like you have no impact, you have complete ownership. As you imagine these contrasting feelings, picture what your corresponding actions would look like and try to act that way. In other words, fake it until you make it. Sometimes shifting your actions first can help your energy and attitude follow them.

- Consider playing a game of role-reversal. Reflect on a person at work who frustrates you and imagine being that person. How might you describe your environment and rationale for your actions and behaviors as the other person? When you take on the role of another person you can often shift your negativity into a more open and compassionate perspective towards them. While this might not completely remove the barrier, it helps you adjust your thinking and attitude, which opens up your ability to find creative solutions and move forward rather than remaining stuck.

- Embrace the belief that everyone is doing the best they can with what they have, and that no one person or thing is intentionally trying to make your work miserable. Then reexamine the aspects of your work that you find frustrating and limiting. Explore ideas for working alongside others to minimize the barriers and create an improved environment in which to achieve. It is quite possible that you are not alone in your frustrations. By choosing to lead an effort to find creative solutions you can open up options for others as well.

- Commit to one day of choosing "positive" in every interaction, and see what happens to your mood, your energy, and your productivity. Choose to do so on more and more days until it becomes a habit.

- When you feel really awful, try looking in the mirror and smiling! I know this might sound crazy, but try it. It is really hard to stay angry, sad, or upset when you see yourself smiling. If nothing else you will laugh at yourself doing such an odd thing! Try taking it up a notch and put a mirror on your desk, always smiling while on the phone. You will be surprised by how different you sound and how the smile transmits over the audible conversation.

Reflection Exercise 23

As you reflect on your attitude, where do you see the greatest opportunity for growth?

Download the Journal at: www.leadershipbychoice.com

4. Low Confidence

Lack of confidence often comes from the inner critic that challenges you and tries to protect you from venturing outside your comfort zone. Your inner critic is that internal voice behind your thoughts that keeps you from speaking, taking action, and moving forward in certain circumstances, acting as a barrier to your success. This can show up in the workplace in ways such as:

- While you are preparing a presentation for your peer group, you notice it's taking significantly longer than it should. You repeatedly change, refine, edit, and adjust the content. In your head you hear, "Who are you to present on this topic?! There are many more qualified than you. You'd better make sure this presentation is perfect to validate why you were chosen to present on this topic."

- You are heading into a meeting you're going to lead and hear, "Be careful; they might see what a phony you are – all talk, no action. You'd better start to walk the talk more."

- You are considering interviewing for a new job in your company and your inner critic says, "You aren't qualified to do that job." Or "There are others far more experienced than you for that job, don't do it." Or "Do you know how *hard* that job will be? Do you really want the added workload and pressure?"

- You want to be considered more of an enthusiastic, forward-looking employee, but you say to yourself,

"You are not organized enough, attractive enough, strong enough, [etc.]."

- You are a staff member who wants to be given leadership opportunities, but you hear, "You can barely make it to the office on time... how will you lead others?" Or "How will you lead your peers? They know so much about you – the good, the bad, and the ugly!"

- You take on a leadership assignment, but all you hear is, "You have never done this before. Who are you to think you can do it? You are no better than anyone else."

- You are sitting in a meeting with your leadership team and have a great idea you believe will help the team advance. As you debate sharing your thought, you hear, "Nah, that's not really anything new and exciting. Keep quiet for now and maybe share it with someone later."

For some of you this inner critic is loud and recognizable. You can relate to wondering if you are truly qualified to do your work, good enough for the job, or smart enough for the next promotion. Everyone has heard their inner critic at one time or another. Perhaps you've worked diligently to put a muzzle on this type of thinking and barely hear it, however it is still there working to protect you, ready to hold you back at times, fueling your thought process.

To gain confidence:
- Learn to recognize your inner critic and acknowledge that it is just trying to protect you from the risks of

taking on a challenge. Embrace your inner critic and bring it with you on the journey.

- Feed your brain with positive affirmations. There is a lot of research showing that the brain responds to what it is told and cannot discern between the stimuli of spoken language and actual actions. If you tell your brain you are a great presenter and an inspirational leader, as with visualization it starts to assume that role and creates feelings of confidence, allowing you to act the part!

- Fake it till you make it! Similar to using this technique to adjust your attitude, you can use it to demonstrate confidence: Stand tall, maintain eye contact in conversations, speak clearly and directly, smile, nod, and listen!

- Identify the skill sets that challenge your confidence the most, and commit to improving in those areas. If presenting to your peers is difficult, create opportunities to present more frequently to both your peer group and others. For example, create round-table discussions in which you have the opportunity to lead and present on a topic of interest, or a professional book group on leadership in which you each have an opportunity to share or present. Start with small groups and expand to bigger ones, adding media and slide presentations and using a microphone to build your confidence and presence over time. Face the very thing that challenges you the most, knowing that the sooner you can master the skill the sooner the fear or discomfort will be a thing of the past.

- Make a list of your accomplishments in all areas of your life. Identify skills you have mastered over the years. Write this as your own private resume, highlighting all you have accomplished including work from high school, college, projects, volunteering efforts, music, the arts, and athletics. Include relationships you have impacted, people you have influenced, and ways you have made differences in the lives of others. Include everything. Celebrate all you have achieved and not what you still hope to achieve; you will address that in the next chapter!

- Accept that you are *perfectly imperfect*, and charge ahead!

- Understand that to grow and develop you may need to endure some discomfort. Remember the athletes – to build muscle they first need to experience small micro-tears in their muscles. You may not feel confident in everything you set out to achieve; however, overcoming this barrier requires you to move forward despite the discomfort. Zig Ziglar, and then John C. Maxwell, shared, "If you wait for all the lights to turn green, you'll never leave the driveway." Overcoming the barrier of low confidence starts with getting out of the driveway first regardless of what lies ahead.

Reflection Exercise 24

As you reflect on your confidence, what is one area in which lack of confidence holds you back? What is one strategy you can commit to to improve your confidence in this particular area?

Download the Journal at: www.leadershipbychoice.com

5. False Assumptions

An expectation or assumption that the past is a predictor of the future causes your thoughts, attitude, energy, and decisions to be impacted by the assumption. This might show up in the workplace as follows:

Topic	Decision	Past experience dictating the decision
Hiring	I will never hire a _____.	The last _____ I hired was unproductive.
Communication	I can't approach my boss with an idea.	She didn't listen to my ideas before.
Attitude	Everything I want requires a fight.	I have had to fight for everything I wanted.
Time/Energy	I can never take on another role.	The last time I tried something new I was stressed out and exhausted.

| Performance | _____ will never meet her quota. | _____ has missed her quota for two quarters. |
| Finances | I won't bother asking for more budget to develop this great program. | My budget requests for new programs last year were denied. |

To challenge false assumptions:

- Dig deep to find a possible false assumption when your options seem limited. Depending on how long you have treated the assumption as a truth, you may not recognize the limitations your assumption has created. For example, I once knew a regional medical-device sales director who was hiring for a critical sales role. He reluctantly spoke with a candidate who was recommended by one of his leading sales representatives. The candidate was extremely successful in all of his previous sales roles, but had no sales experience in medical devices specifically. Everything about the candidate matched the job requirements. Based on a previous bad experience, the director believed that people without prior medical-device sales experience were not capable of doing the job. He didn't hire him for that reason. (His competitor did, however, and the region had to compete against his stellar sales performance for years.)

- Realize that just because it happened that way in the past does not mean it will happen that way in the future. In the second example above, recognize that just because your boss did not like your idea the first time does not guarantee a similar response to a new idea at a different time. You might be hesitant to approach her; however, consider using the original experience to openly communicate your assumptions and concerns about approaching her with ideas. There is a good possibility that you will both benefit from having an open dialogue.

- Consider outcomes other than what your assumption forecasts, and what opportunities could open up if the assumption were false. For example, in the "Finances" example in the table above, rather than not submitting a budget request at all, imagine what you would request if you believed multiple requests would be approved? Just by shifting this thought you allow for creative thinking. When you contemplate alternative scenarios you open your mind to possibility and gradually challenge the false assumption that is getting in your way of moving forward.

- Decide not to let the past dictate your future. When you recognize that you are treating a past experience as a predictor of a future outcome, you are *choosing* to let the past dictate the future. In other words, there is no guarantee that what happened yesterday will happen again today, and as long as you believe it will, and therefore intercept it before it can repeat, you will never have the opportunity to see a different result and realize the full potential of a different outcome. You can rationalize it in this way, or simply make a choice that regardless of what happened in the past you will treat each situation on its own merits and not allow your past experience to restrict your ability to assess, evaluate, and consider alternatives moving forward. I am not suggesting you ignore your past experiences, as there is a lot to learn from them; I am suggesting that you recognize when a false assumption is preventing you from exploring all options and thus limiting your ability to move closer to achieving your goal.

Reflection Exercise 25

As you reflect on false assumptions, is there one that is holding you back today? In what different ways might you view this assumption?

Download the Journal at: www.leadershipbychoice.com

6. Restricting Beliefs

You might harbor concepts, ideas, or thoughts that you have always accepted as truth or "the way it is," and therefore you have never really challenged them. Gender-related beliefs fall into this category of restricting beliefs. Not considering all options as a result of such beliefs can certainly limit your growth. Examples of restricting beliefs include:

- You can't be a good partner/mother/father and be successful at your job; something must give – there is no such thing as balance.

- You have to have a college degree to be an effective, competent leader.

- Younger workers work harder than older workers.

- Older workers are more experienced and therefore are better managers.

- Success is about making money.

- Being a leader is hard.

- Leaders are tough.

- Success takes hard work.

Restricting beliefs also show up in more subtle ways by influencing choices we make subconsciously, so it is helpful to invest time in challenging beliefs that might be holding you back. Your beliefs impact how you choose to lead, communicate, hire, develop, and judge those around you. For example, if you believe that older workers bring hands-on experience and tremendous value to an organization and make strong leaders, you will contribute to a culture that supports older employees. If you believe that older workers are past their prime, out of touch, and unable to provide cutting-edge thinking, your actions and decisions will contribute to a culture that supports young workers. Like false assumptions, in many situations restricting beliefs are so ingrained in habitual patterns that acknowledging them as potential barriers can be challenging.

Restricting beliefs hinder our efforts towards and attitudes about reaching goals, and make us feel inadequate. For many years people believed that women were not mathematically inclined and therefore not well suited for roles in engineering and the sciences. As a woman who excelled in math from an early age, and who presently works with both men and women in STEM-related fields (science, technology, engineering, and math), it is evident to me that this belief directly and indirectly influenced women's choices whether or not to pursue careers in these fields. Fortunately schools aggressively worked to change this perception, thereby opening up possibilities for young boys and girls and men and women as they pursue their professional aspirations, benefitting all of society.

Another perfect example of a restricting belief was the longstanding acceptance that running a mile in under four minutes was impossible for a human. It was believed and accepted as truth, even by doctors and scientists, that the body would collapse under the exertion, so it was never even considered as a goal until Sir Roger Bannister decided to try it in 1954.

With his eyes and training on the goal, another elite runner, John Landy, from Australia, also sought that goal. On May 6th, 1954, Bannister had his chance, and probably his last one, to break the record, as Landy was scheduled to run in the upcoming weeks. Despite the cold, wet, and windy day – everything working against him – Bannister ran the first three-quarters of a mile in just over 3 minutes, an average of 60 seconds per lap. He needed to do the last lap in 59 seconds, and he made history that day, which he knew was his only chance, running the mile in 3:59.4 minutes.

Forty-six days later Landy beat his time, followed by more and more people who broke the four-minute mile once they realized it was possible. For years it had never been achieved, yet as soon as the belief barrier was broken – the opportunity now a possibility, others achieved it.

To challenge restricting beliefs:
1. Pick one of your beliefs that relates to your role as a leader and seems pretty concrete.

2. Focus on what it would mean for you if it were not true.

3. Examine how this belief might be limiting you.

4. Consider how you might approach your role if you believed something different?

5. Consider the belief from another angle or perspective to see if it really holds water.

6. Determine whether the belief is actually true or you can replace it with a more realistic one.

Banister chose to challenge the belief that it was impossible to run a mile in under four minutes. In so doing he actually created the possibility. Had he held on to the existing belief he would never have trained with the expectation of achieving the goal, thereby limiting himself. Believing something different freed him to create a training routine to accomplish that goal. In regard to the physiology, I cannot speak to whether he looked at it from another angle, but I suspect he reflected on the many times that other records were beaten and surpassed despite beliefs that such feats were impossible.

Reflection Exercise 26

Take a moment to list some restricting beliefs you have today. What is a completely opposite view, and how would that belief impact your thoughts and actions moving forward?

Download the Journal at: www.leadershipbychoice.com

7. Fear of Success or Failure

Fear is possibly the greatest barrier to success. It's ironic that fear of success is as much a problem as fear of failure. While the initial barrier may be the fear of trying something and failing, there can be equal fear of further responsibilities after accomplishing your goal. If you don't try, there is no way you can fail, and you won't even have to think about what comes next if you were to succeed.

Even if you have well-thought-out goals and dreams for yourself and your career you can be paralyzed with indecision. Fueled by your inner critic, you remain unable to shift or change your course. Underlying this is fear that can show up as:

- Fear of being vulnerable by communicating your heart's desire

- Fear that if you share your dreams someone will shoot them down or even laugh at them (and you)

- Fear of the unknown – that you don't know where you'll be if you go for it and it doesn't work out

- Fear that if you succeed you won't be able to meet the challenges of your success

In reflecting on the journey of starting my own company and creating a life that truly honors my talents and passions, I would be lying if I told you I had no fear. I worked hard to remove my fear and stay focused on my vision, but I definitely experienced fear:

- I was afraid of doing it and not being able to bring all the pieces together to make it a viable business.

- I was afraid that others would think, "This will never happen."

- I was afraid of losing time with friends.

- I was afraid of not having the skills needed to run a business.

- I was afraid of losing financial stability.

- I was afraid that my dream might be just a phase I was going through.

- I was afraid that if I succeeded in creating a thriving, growing business it might not actually fit my vision and I might not love it.

To minimize your fear:

- Going back to your core values, tap into why you want to achieve your goal to begin with. When you can truly embrace your "why" – a larger purpose, higher calling, whatever it may be – fear becomes a distant and flickering thought as you are more readily able to understand that achieving this goal is more important than your fear.

- Ask yourself, "What is the worst thing that could happen if I fail (or succeed)?" Explore that until it's no longer insurmountable, then tackle another "worst thing" and another until you've neutralized your fear of undesirable consequences. In Dale Carnegie's book *How to Stop Worrying and Start Living*, he reveals how to handle a worst possible outcome by simply devising a solution for it ahead of time. Then the fear of it happening loses its power over you, freeing you to move beyond it and take positive action.

- Remember that you are never alone and that there are always people available to support you.

- Consider that your dreams come from deep within you – gifts from God, the universe, or your higher power. And if you're able to dream it you most likely have the strength and ability from the same source to make the dream a reality. Remembering that you are part of something greater than yourself can help wash away fears.

Reflection Exercise 27

What is the biggest fear you face today? How would you work differently without the fear?

Download the Journal at: www.leadershipbychoice.com

8. Poor Relationship with Time

Lacking the skill set to put a reasonable and time-oriented plan in place creates a myriad of obstacles in the workplace, and failing to organize around even a marginally good plan can do so as well. You might have a tremendous vision, fully aligned values, and a great team, but without a plan, a timeline, and some organization your vision will likely fall short. The old adage *"Failing to plan is planning to fail"* definitely gets to the heart of it. Having poor relationships with time, planning, and organization can result in:

- Failing to meet deadlines

- Failing to meet forecasts

- Having a vision and clear goals but always falling short in one or two areas

- Continually having the same goals on your list with no forward progress

- Being consistently over or under budget

- Not being able to fit everything you need to accomplish into your day/week/month

- Constantly "losing" or misplacing paperwork, electronic files, and objects important to your tasks

- Always being under pressure to complete an urgent task, sometimes working crazy hours to do so

While all of the above points are the result of poor time management, planning, or organizational skills, the greatest barrier is the mindset these create. My clients who are challenged with this obstacle often translate the corresponding outcomes with a negative thought process such as:

- I need more time.

- I'm never on time.

- I don't know how to meet deadlines.

- I'm unreliable.

- I'm incompetent.

- I can't get out of my own way.

- I'm a failure.

- I'm so disorganized.

- I'm always stressed out.

- I can't, I don't, I'm not… [etc.].

When my clients need help with timelines and the pressure of their workload, which is quite common, it's interesting to find that the problem is less a result of the workload than of poor planning or poor time management. The great news is that tangible tools for solutions are readily available, and new skill sets can be learned.

Strategies for managing a poor relationship with time:

Honest self-assessment is key to developing effective strategies to compensate for poor time management, planning, and organization. If this area is not your particular strength, there are endless options for support based on your preference, such as smartphone apps, written materials and planners, and creative organizational systems. Combined with minor refinements in daily systems, any of these can go a long way in improving your skills! For some, however, outside assistance from others is the solution. In addition to creative tools and resources readily available, there are incredible people who eat, sleep, and breathe planning and organization and who would be honored to work with you and support you! It does not matter *how* this barrier is addressed, only that you improve your relationship with time and organizational skills as much as possible, as poor planning and organization can stall forward progress in your personal life as well as at your workplace. Here are some ideas:

- Keep a precise journal of your day, for a week or at least several days, capturing everything you do from the moment you wake up until the moment you go to sleep. Record the event and the time it takes. Then review it to see where you can tweak your schedule to get more out of it.

- Start your day with a written plan for each segment of your time, with the times entered in a column. At the end of your day, account for how true to your plan you were able to stay, noting in a right-hand column where your planned time and actual time deviated. Continue to work on this until your planned days and actual days begin to mirror each other.

- Schedule a one-hour non-negotiable appointment with yourself at the end of each week to review the following week's plan. Be sure to block off additional time before and after each appointment and meeting for preparation, commuting, and follow-up. We often forget to schedule these important activities, contributing to a lot of stressful rushing around.

- Use a more detailed project-scheduling system than you currently employ. For example, if your presentation is one month away, schedule weekly milestones to accomplish on your calendar rather than making just the one entry for next month and having that "Oh shucks!" moment a week before the presentation.

- Keep an electronic version of your calendar on your smartphone, or if that isn't working go back to pen and paper. Studies repeatedly support that the physical art of writing commits more to memory than the act of typing.

- Review your schedule and identify what you truly control and what you do not – prioritize and adjust accordingly.

- Track your planning accuracy and GET REALLY HONEST with yourself. Do you consistently think a four-hour project will only take one hour? Adjust your timing expectations and get real.

- Review some of the applications for smartphones designed to assist the busy professional: Mile IQ, Dragon Dictation, Expensify, Hours, Waze, and Google Maps, to name only a fraction of the multitude of options.

- Choose one thing that will have a significant impact on either your schedule or how you organize it, and implement it – only one. When you've made that a habit, move on to one idea at a time until your skill set is working well. Don't overwhelm yourself with an all-or-nothing approach. Every little change helps move you closer to the goal.

- Ask a trusted friend or colleague for assistance.

- Invest in a trained executive assistant to help you stay organized and on schedule, freeing you up to do the work you do best.

Everyone has the same twenty-four hours in each day. Once that time is over, it is never yours for the taking again. Choosing to work on your relationship with time allows you to spend it on that which is necessary and is of most importance to you. While each of the above options can help improve your scheduling, they do not address *how* you are choosing to spend your time. When you are not spending your time on what matters most to you, your thoughts can spiral into negativity, further contributing to this barrier. To ensure you are investing your twenty-four hours focused on what matters to you most, I suggest taking a step back altogether and design, if you will, your "ideal week."

Ideal Week

Returning to your core values and vision, schedule your ideal week in order of your priorities. Do not allow all of your tasks and responsibilities to take precedence on this calendar. This exercise helps you align your days more closely with your ideal. Some of the following might be priorities that you typically neglect when scheduling your time:

- Meditation, prayer, or reflection

- Exercise and fitness

- Quality time with loved ones, family, and friends

- Work and travel

- Growth and development

- Planning

- Down time – relaxing, reading, television, movies, games

- Household projects

If one week is too short of a time frame for scheduling your responsibilities, try the ideal month. For example, you might schedule one weekend each month for a specific family adventure, or one weekend for travel or a sporting event, or one weekend to focus on home projects. Enjoy the process of prioritizing how you spend your time so that you can improve your relationship to time and teach yourself how to work with it instead of it working against you.

What is one strategy you would like to employ to improve your relationship with time?

Reflection Exercise 28

Examine your relationship with time.
Plan your ideal week and month.

Download the Journal at: www.leadershipbychoice.com

9. Lack of Accountability

Without accountability it is almost impossible to move action forward in a timely fashion. Accountability provides checkpoints and opportunities to measure and evaluate progress towards a desired goal. Just as with poor planning and organization, lack of accountability holds you back, contributes to feeling irresponsible and inadequate, and fosters self-doubt. It is directly tied to achieving forward progress and timely results towards a goal. Ignoring this necessary measure puts a barrier between your vision and achieving success.

Despite knowing this, holding yourself and others accountable to expectations can be challenging. To do so on a personal level requires intense discipline. To do so with others requires providing feedback on a regular basis, which can be uncomfortable when the necessary feedback is negative or contrary. So rather than provide feedback, the tendency is to avoid it and hope the issue will go away or that someone else will deal with it. In some instances you might rationalize that the negative performance isn't really that bad, and that it isn't worth the confrontation, thereby rationalizing away the need to give feedback. You can have a great plan and timeline, and superior organization, yet fail to hold yourself and others accountable for meeting expectations and timelines. Failure to do so affects overall performance, trust, and confidence. Here are some ways this shows up in the workplace:

- You rationalize missing deadlines – there is always a viable reason. Often it is simply due to your extensive workload and a "something must give" rationale.

- There is one member on your team who seems to be a bottleneck for others in missed deadlines or incomplete work, slowing overall project completion, yet you don't address the issue and expect the rest of your team to compensate for this person. Months may pass and this employee continues to underperform.

- You are consistently over budget, requiring others to reduce spending in their departments, which sends the message that it is okay to overspend.

- Meetings start only after everyone rolls in, sometimes ten to fifteen minutes past the scheduled start time.

- Your projections rarely match your results, sending the message that you are disconnected from the business in some capacity.

- During regularly scheduled meetings there is little or no follow-up on previous decisions, commitments, and action items, allowing projects and action items to linger on, disappear, and fall off the schedule for completion.

- There are no regularly scheduled meetings. You simply meet when necessary.

- There is little or no scheduled time to give and receive feedback with supervisors and those who report to you.

- On a personal level you have great vision for the work you want to accomplish, but feel desperately behind in every aspect. Other than identifying the project or goal, you have made limited progress.

- You have professional-development objectives that continually get pushed off your calendar.

- You make promises to follow through on tasks but often don't.

- Others commit to completing tasks or projects but continually miss their stated deadlines.

Addressing lack of accountability:

Creating an environment of accountability requires regularly scheduled opportunities to both give and receive feedback. Unfortunately conversations with colleagues about accountability usually occur only when something is missing, late, incomplete, or negative, or the project is in crisis mode. If all is moving along smoothly, there is a perception that there is no need for a meeting. This is not dissimilar to how many leaders work with their direct reports, thus creating an environment of uneasiness when their staff members are asked to meet with them. Most people don't enjoy receiving negative feedback, and as a result they avoid situations in which they have the responsibility to be the deliverer of negative feedback.

By scheduling regular meetings for accountability and check-ins, you set up a continual, open environment for both positive and negative feedback, not just negative feedback. Keeping the heart and intention of the feedback in the forefront is what differentiates accountability meetings. When your intention is to genuinely help the other person achieve a goal, or help the team stay on track of a project to facilitate success, both positive and negative feedback is received favorably.

While delivering and receiving negative feedback can be unpleasant, I have found that most people prefer knowing how they might be falling short in order to have an opportunity to resolve the issue. I have always preferred knowing exactly where I stand for just that reason. On the other side of it, I also prefer to be candid with someone when I have identified a disconnect, affording us the opportunity to resolve the problem and continue to move closer to the goal.

The most successful leaders I know make time weekly or semimonthly to meet and connect with their teams to review objectives and progress. While this requires time, it proves to be invaluable. That time to connect keeps the goal in sight, helps steer and focus activity, and fosters positive accountability and ultimate success. In the military we used the expression "inspect what you expect." By keeping a regular cadence of reviewing goals, expectations, and progress towards the goals, you help maintain focus, clarity, and success.

As disciplined as I believe I am, I always experienced my greatest weeks in sales when I was working with my manager, training new sales representatives, or in the week leading up to a monthly check-in or accountability call. While I would like to think that my work ethic and intensity was the same on every day, I was always more productive and fruitful when accountability of some format was involved. Weekly calls with my manager forced me to regularly review my progress each week and evaluate areas for improvement. The calls helped me maintain focus and truly impacted my ability to reach my personal goals, and as a group we were able to reach our team goals. It is far better for your reputation and your team's reputation to demonstrate and report progress than not to. Accountability drives performance, and performance fuels confidence for all.

Accountability Drives Success

There are several well-known examples of how accountability contributes to achieving successful outcomes. For example:

Weight Watchers, considered one of the most successful and longstanding weight-loss programs, first differentiated itself by incorporating weekly meetings and weigh-ins for their participants. This created a positive environment of accountability. Knowing that you would be weighed each week in front of at least one person contributed to taking greater responsibility and being more dedicated to reaching your goal. Each week participants receive feedback and openly review their progress with a counselor. They review their goals from the prior week; their food and activity diaries; and their mindset, challenges, and successes. Next they set new goals and review potential obstacles that might get in their way during the following week, with the hope that by anticipating potential obstacles they will be better prepared to navigate them, minimizing any negative impact they could have. For example, if they will be attending a social event one evening, they plan their food choices for earlier in the day to allow for some treats that evening. This weekly accountability has contributed to the successful achievement of desired weight-loss goals in men and women for over fifty years.

Personal fitness training works in a similar fashion. Numerous driven and self-motivated people have found that despite being fairly disciplined regarding their workouts, they are more committed when they have a personal trainer to whom they are accountable on a weekly basis to review their workouts and progress. By working with a trainer who is an expert in their field, you are able to review your progress and challenges and make adjustments in your workouts, setting you up for successful accomplishment of your fitness goals. Similar to Weight Watchers, the results are completely dependent on your choices, commitment, and activity; however, your counselor or trainer is there to hold you accountable, to be a resource, and to guide you to keep you on track.

Coaching is another form of accountability for leaders. Similar to having fitness goals, many professionals today are identifying developmental career and leadership aspirations for themselves and seeking coaching for guidance and accountability. After establishing clear goals and objectives, a plan is put in place with weekly or semimonthly calls for accountability. The coach and the client review progress, celebrate successes, review barriers, and identify solutions for forward progress. Similar to Weight Watchers, coaches help plan for upcoming events that pose either an obstacle to or an opportunity for continued progress towards achieving the client's goals, and strategically coach around the topics.

Being highly driven and focused, I initially viewed business and leadership coaching as a great resource for those needing an extra boost in support, motivation, and outside encouragement, and for those needing someone else to hold them accountable and show them the way. I saw this as a critical service for my company to provide, knowing that I planned to be working with leaders, and therefore embarked on becoming certified in the field for the sole purpose of better understanding the practice for others. I was seriously underestimating the value of coaching! It's not only for the aforementioned. It was in my personal experience working with a business coach that I recognized an explosive growth in my business and in my ability to set lofty goals and achieve them. Having weekly accountability calls with an experienced business and Energy Leadership coach has been a key differentiator in the success of my new business.

Personal Accountability

It is clear to me that the highly accomplished people I work with value accountability. Without it you can allow a barrier to slow or prevent your forward progress towards reaching goals in a timely fashion. One of the very first questions I ask my clients is "How do you want to be held accountable?"

In regard to your own accountability, ask yourself the same question. In regard to your performance, ask yourself, "Would I put up with my behavior from someone who works for me?" If the answer is no, consider being a bit harder on yourself. You are your own boss whether you run your company or not. Treat yourself as your most valuable employee and hold yourself accountable as if the success of your company depends exclusively on doing your job well and being accountable for completing your portion of the work.

Reflection Exercise 29

How do you like to hold yourself accountable? What strategies can you adopt to remain accountable and achieve more for yourself?

Download the Journal at: www.leadershipbychoice.com

10. Lack of Communication

Strong communication skills are integral to helping prevent and work through several different kinds of barriers. Poor communication is often behind an ill-informed opinion or interpretation of a situation, which then creates its own brand of roadblock, confounding your efforts to reach a goal. A significant number of my clients have had to admit that their incorrect interpretations were the result of not listening appropriately or not communicating effectively, such as:

- My boss thinks I'm demanding.

- She doesn't like my style of communication.

- He doesn't want any more responsibility.

- My team thinks I'm unreasonable.

- My clients don't want to hear from me.

- Salespeople are a pain.

- My boss is always short-tempered with me and must hate me.

- He's always running late and clearly doesn't care about us or his work.

- She thinks I'm not qualified for my role. You can tell by the way she talks to me.

- She thinks I'm overqualified for my role.

- Our pricing is too high for that client.

Interpretations and poor communication can spiral endlessly, having a direct impact on your thoughts and choices. Each misinterpretation can foster an action that leads to another misinterpretation, and the cycle continues.

Communication:
Cycle of Interpretations

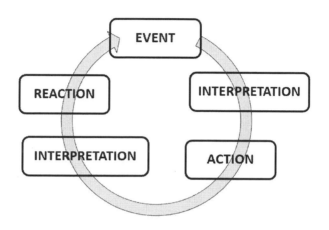

Imagine the following scenario:

Event: Bill repeatedly shows up late for work.

Jane's interpretation: "Bill doesn't care about his work. He is always running late."

Choice/Action: Jane doesn't feel Bill is reliable, so she chooses to share less work with him.

Bill's interpretation: "Jane never delegates. She thinks she is the only one who can do the work – so full of herself!"

Choice/Reaction: Bill chooses to distance himself from Jane, since clearly she doesn't respect or value him.

Event: Bill is not only still late for meetings, but now even more distant and disengaged.

Jane's interpretation: "Bill *really* doesn't care about his work at all anymore. In fact, he is completely unreliable. I am so tired of working with incompetent people."

...and the cycle continues.

To minimize communication problems:

- Pause when you find yourself assuming you understand the intent and motivation behind an event. Before jumping to conclusions, consider having an honest and candid conversation directly with the person. In the scenario above, a conversation between Bill and Jane could have quickly filled in the gaps; provided the opportunity to communicate expectations and interpretations of each other's actions; and allowed for a viable understanding and resolution. Both parties are responsible for initiating such a conversation. Regardless of the hierarchy, consider reaching out in a professional manner to gain understanding any time a situation or relationship feels challenging.

- Take a breath and think about alternative ways to view the situation. In the scenario above, what reasons could there be for Bill being consistently late other than he doesn't care about his work? Perhaps Bill's commute is unpredictable. Perhaps he meets with a colleague in another department each morning to work on a special project and is actually at work an hour early in order to do so. Maybe he is managing a personal family matter that he prefers not to discuss at work. The possibilities are endless, and until Jane has an honest conversation with Bill about it, jumping to conclusions is creating barriers for both parties.

- Consider viewing the situation from another colleague's perspective (without asking, as you don't want to be perceived as unprofessional or catty). One of my clients felt her boss hated her because he was always short-tempered with her. I challenged her to describe how another colleague might describe their boss. She admitted that his description would be similar in that their boss was short-tempered with him as well, but that he would also say that it has nothing to do with the boss liking him or not, but more to do with the pressure and workload he believes their boss faces.

- Consider a completely opposite point of view and construct possible actions consistent with that view. One of my clients felt like a loyal customer didn't want to hear from him and my client was reluctant to reach out for follow-up and possible referrals. I suggested this tactic, and upon imagining that his client absolutely wanted to hear from him and would be honored to give him referrals based on the exceptional work he had provided for her, he confidently reached out for follow-up. He quickly realized he had created a barrier based on poor communication. It was his thoughts getting in his way, creating a barrier to his success. Not only did he learn a valuable lesson, but he added several referrals, leading to more business for his team.

- Try putting yourself in the other person's shoes and imagine what you think they might say about the same situation. By shifting your focus to an alternative interpretation from the perspective of the other party, you can work around poor communication and open up avenues for greater communication and understanding.

- Challenge yourself to seek direct, face-to-face communication whenever possible. The single most effective way to gain clarity about a situation or event is to have a two-way, in-person conversation. In other words, not a conversation via email, text, or Snapchat – a real conversation in which eye contact, tone of voice, heart, and body language are communicated. Using sincere, direct, and non-threatening language (avoiding generalizations and language such as "You always…" and "You never…") combined with a heart of genuine curiosity and concern, your efforts at direct communication will create pathways instead of barriers.

Rather than allowing your thoughts and corresponding actions to prevent you from achieving your goals, consider going directly to the source to provide clarity, peace of mind, and opportunity for impact.

Reflection Exercise 30

Consider one person you work with today with whom you would like to have a heartfelt, open dialogue. What would you like to achieve in this conversation, and how will it help support your goals and vision moving forward?

Download the Journal at: www.leadershipbychoice.com

Pull It Together

The key to overcoming barriers is to accept that they are real and present for everyone, so they will naturally try to block your road to leadership as well. The challenge is in learning to identify them quickly and using strategies to break through them. Look at the barrier as if it's actually an *opportunity* to move you closer to your goal, strengthening your character along the way. Whether it's a person, a task, or an organizational element, see the obstacle as a game or puzzle specifically put in your path to help you master maintaining a strong, positive attitude despite adversity. Although it's certainly not a game, I have found that compartmentalizing it as such can help remove the emotional element attached to the block, freeing up your energy and attitude so you can be more productive as you work to solve the "puzzle" or win the "game." The faster you can do so the faster you can get back on the road to becoming the leader you want to be. Consider this tale of two Olympians:

Great Britain's Mohamed Farah was the highly anticipated gold medalist runner in the 10,000 meter race in the 2014 Olympics. He had won it once already, and a second win would be the first time anyone achieved two golds for this event. Early in the race, through no fault of anyone, he tumbled and fell, putting him far out of lead position.

Canada's Brian McKeever, a cross country skier, was also expected to take the gold in 2014, for the 1KM race. Shortly after the race began he caught an edge and fell, placing him far behind the other competitors.

Both these fine athletes pulled themselves up, continued to race hard, and won gold medals. And Brian McKeever's win was at the Paralympics, the Olympics for athletes with a range of disabilities, as he is legally blind and relies on his brother as his guide.

Their wins were not in whether or not they fell but in how quickly they got up, put themselves back in the race, and stayed focused on their vision – truly an inspiration for me. A mantra I like to remember when faced with barriers is:

It is not if I fall, but in how quickly I get up.

When is the last time you "fell"? How quickly were you able to get up? Think of a time when you felt successful achieving a goal despite being faced with adversity. Recall your attitude and overall mindset. Think about the skill set associated with the achievement. You either already possessed these skills or developed them while going after the goal. Reflect on the planning and execution, the timeline, and accountability. These are all factors that contribute to successfully reaching a goal. Learn to recognize how frequently you have used these skills with ease and how great it felt doing so.

Reflection Exercise 31

Describe a time when you accomplished a goal despite being faced with adversity. What contributed to your ability to do so?

Download the Journal at: www.leadershipbychoice.com

Put It into Practice

One of the greatest rewards of the work I do is in watching clients overcome barriers and achieve goals they felt were impossible. You might wonder why successful, driven, and motivated clients seek coaching. It's because they are driven to learn more; achieve more; increase their efficiency; raise their awareness; and broaden their reach, influence, and impact. And they know the value of being accountable to someone specifically trained to help them get out of their own way, identify their barriers, and expeditiously move forward to reach new goals they have set for themselves.

Excited to follow up with me, a participant in one of my workshop series named Shubha shared her personal journal entry with me after attending the program. I did not know about her goal, and upon reading her entry I was reminded how powerful having a vision and an awareness of barriers – and a strategy for overcoming them – can help you reach far! Here's her account:

Rejection to Acceptance, One Mailbox at a Time

I always told everyone around me that I am not a runner. "Even if a big tiger chases me, maybe I will run for three seconds before lying on the ground offering myself as a juicy meal to the tiger," I would say. I was not physically weak. I scaled Half Dome in Yosemite after carrying my supplies and tent for days. I have hiked and camped backcountry. I have tried CrossFit. I have biked for hundreds of miles. But I said I couldn't run.

One day I asked myself, "Why am I not a runner?" I had no answer. Maybe I was afraid of failure and had convinced myself that I couldn't run. My friend Erin gently coaxed me to try. I gave up mentally every time I tried. "I am not a runner," I kept telling myself. I just couldn't visualize myself running.

I made a small goal. Not a goal to run, but a goal to visualize myself running. Then for two months I did nothing but imagine myself running. One morning I started running on the sidewalk. That first day my run lasted twenty seconds. My second day it was thirty seconds. After two weeks I still couldn't run for more than a minute.

I started realizing that my body still had a lot of energy, but my mind kept telling me I was tired. The third week of running, when I wanted to stop, I pushed myself to run to one mailbox ahead of me on the sidewalk. It was a small but achievable goal. Every time I reached a mailbox, I pushed myself to run to the next mailbox. Finally I was running!

The day before the race, when Erin asked me if I was ready, I was not but I did it anyway. I stopped my gremlins (inner critic) for forty minutes and I ran. I did my first 5k. I turned my own rejection ("I am not a good runner") to acceptance ("I am working to become a better runner").

I am very thankful for having such wonderful friends who believe in me more than I believe in myself!

In a few short months Shubha was able to challenge her barriers and accomplish the goal of becoming a runner. She created a vision, challenged her beliefs, muzzled her inner critic, reframed her attitude and energy, and succeeded.

When you are faced with barriers, view them as exercises designed to build your strength and endurance as a leader, such as:

1. Strengthening your alignment with your values

2. Building clarity around your vision

3. Exercising your positive energy and attitude

4. Building your confidence

5. Realigning false assumptions

6. Breathing new life into restricting beliefs

7. Pushing away fear

8. Adding cadence to your relationship with time

9. Practicing accountability daily

10. Committing to consistent, direct communication

Like the athlete, embrace that through rigorous training you can build your strength and endurance, preparing for the more demanding leadership roles and opportunities that lie ahead of you.

Reflection Exercise 32

APPLICATION: Go back to the list you created in Reflection Exercise 20 regarding what is holding you back from being the leader you aspire to be. Identify the barrier associated with each item and develop a strategy to work through the barrier and propel yourself forward.

Download the Journal at: www.leadershipbychoice.com

PART II

The Motion:
Create the Momentum

Be the leader you choose to be.

Everyone deserves to work for a great leader, starting with you. Or let me rephrase this to make it a bit clearer: Everyone deserves to work for a great leader, starting with **you** *as your own leader*.

While you may believe that your supervisor is your leader, it is actually you. And before we explore leadership at any other level, let's look at you to understand how you currently lead yourself. In other words, if you were considering hiring you as your boss, would you?

I recently polled several seasoned professionals about their favorite leaders. These people had fifteen years' minimum work experience and had worked for or with no fewer than six managers over the course of their careers. The question was simple:

> "Describe what you most remember or appreciate about leaders you currently work for or have worked for in the past. Please do not give it much thought; I am curious about what comes to mind without any preparation on your part."

It's interesting that the respondents often used "we," referencing the entire team, versus "I":

- He believed in me, and for that I had even a greater desire to do well, grow, and help and support him and the team goals.

- We always knew where we stood with her. She never held back being straight with us. And while we may not have always liked what she had to say, we knew she cared, and that was why she was being up front.

- He was open and honest, sometimes even admitting he didn't have all the answers.

- Despite our long hours and hard work, we always took time to celebrate and laugh. We had fun working together.

- We knew we could go to our manager no matter how difficult the question or how wrong we may have been. She would listen and always find creative solutions for our problems and challenges with our customers.

- She never asked us to do anything she wouldn't do herself or be willing to work together on. She inspired me to want to follow in her footsteps.

- He always asked me about my family, and never forgot anything I shared. I could tell he was genuinely interested in me as a person, not just as his employee.

- He demonstrated confidence and humility simultaneously.

- He created vision, and one I could personally connect to and was confident we could achieve. He was inspiring.

- He was approachable, took time to listen, and created space to hear and interact on a personal and professional level with me.

- She understood the value of personal and professional growth and development, practiced it personally, and made it a part of our every discussion.

- She had clear expectations and held me accountable to high standards. She was not afraid to address missed goals head-on and to raise the bar to challenge me a bit more, and a bit more.

- He made us feel like a winning team and that nothing was out of our reach if we put our heads together and supported each other.

In summary, leaders who are respected, remembered, and appreciated:

- Are confident

- Have integrity and values

- Share vision

- Embrace obstacles

- Listen

- Communicate directly

- Develop and train

- Take time to think

- Hold people accountable

- Praise and recognize

- Celebrate and have fun

- Are inspirational

- Genuinely care

- Create a winning attitude

Take time to think of your own list. What do you value in the leaders you have worked with? Is it similar to what my respondents listed? Based on what you value in a leader, how do you measure up in evaluating yourself as your own boss? Would you want to work for you? Would prior managers rehire you? For you to have impact and influence in the workplace

– to lead, people have to want to hire you, work for you, and work with you every day, regardless of your role or title in your organization! In fact, they would most likely follow you to any organization you chose to be a part of.

Regardless of the size of the organization or role, I have come to appreciate this fundamental principle attributed to Theodore Roosevelt:

People don't care how much you know until they
know how much you care.

So far you have had the opportunity to reflect on your core values, create a vision, assess your attitude, and build your awareness of barriers that can slow you down. Next we will look at the three best ways to demonstrate how much you care:

1. Develop people.
2. Praise and recognize people.
3. Listen to people.

Imagine that your compensation and evaluation as a leader was directly tied to your success in the above three categories. Approach them as if you were to receive a report card in each one. If you genuinely want to make a difference without any change in your job, title, role, or company, I challenge you to adopt this thinking.

In the next three chapters I invite you to explore these three key areas of practice that I believe can exponentially improve your leadership impact right now. As you embrace these practices you will create a momentum in your environment of positive influence on everyone with whom you work and interact.

Reflection Exercise 33

Describe what you most remember or appreciate about leaders you currently work for or have worked for in the past.

Download the Journal at: www.leadershipbychoice.com

CHAPTER 5

Dive into Development

I remember listening to motivational books on cassette tapes early in my career as a salesperson, in my car – yes, *cassette tapes*. I traveled regularly from Rochester, New York, to Jamestown, New York. Without cell phones, and often traveling very early in the morning when even if I had a cell phone I would have been hard-pressed to find someone awake to talk to, I used the time to fuel my development. A great friend of mine and high-achieving and successful sales professional had an entire library of precisely labeled tapes that he shared with me proudly. Listening to those tapes, many of which are listed in "References and Inspirations," my growth journey was in full gear.

I had an insatiable desire to learn from the best – from anyone who had mastered selling, presenting, negotiating, or leading. Coming directly from the military with a degree in mathematics, I was desperately afraid that I was behind all the other salespeople in career development, and therefore felt the need to layer my training to make up for my perceived deficits.

It was during one of those road trips that I first heard about "dressing the part of the next level" and to "assume the role, right now, of the level you aspire to." The speaker continued sharing details along the line of "Wear the clothes, learn the language, observe the skill sets, and if you don't have them, learn them, practice them, and become them." The message I grasped was *"Be the leader today that you want to be tomorrow."* It should not surprise me, although it does, that over twenty years ago, while driving in my first company car on the New York State Thruway, the seed was being planted for this very book – my vision and desire for each of you!

One of the first lessons I learned while training to sell medical devices was the importance of asking open-ended questions. The purpose was to uncover the true needs of the customer, and then I could pull from the data in my brain the features and benefits that would meet the client's need and win the sale – at least I *hoped* I would be able to choose the right features and benefits, carefully selected from weeks of memorizing lists for each surgical product and surgical procedure in both our product line and those of the competition.

The reality was that while the client was answering my first strategically prepared question that I had pondered and created while driving sixty miles to the appointment, rather than actually listening to the answer I desperately needed to hear I was already thinking of my next question and furiously scanning my brain for the appropriately filed answer, unable to hear anything the client was saying. Over time the conversations got easier and my ability to truly listen and respond appropriately came naturally.

Knowledge Builds Confidence

What changed? I gained confidence – confidence that I knew what I needed to know to answer any question or objection that might come my way, confidence in the products I represented, and confidence in the sales process and who I was as a salesperson. The confidence came from both experience and knowledge. I was growing and developing, the result of choices I consciously made to ensure my ability to do and be my best. I owned and embraced any and every opportunity to work towards being better, fueled by desperately wanting to succeed and prove (to myself and to my inner critic that was challenging me) in some fashion that despite not having prior sales experience I was fully qualified to do the job.

Of all of the barriers to success, your inner critic seems to always be present. That faint voice questioning whether you are good enough or smart enough lurks ever so persistently. As you continue to invest in your development and expertise, that voice becomes less audible and your confidence builds.

Consider the work you do today. Unless you are relatively new in your role, I suspect a fair amount of it comes easily to you. You have likely been doing it for years, you know the technical aspects, you know how to communicate about it, and you don't give it a thought – you simply show up to work and do. Now think back to when you first started this type of work – everything from establishing the best route to drive to work to the actual skill set required and the reporting system you needed to learn. There was a lot to think about. Your ability to be available to others, listen, and be fully present was less than it is now. Things that originally required a great deal of thought and processing are now like riding a bicycle – once you learn and master it, you never have to give it a second thought. You no longer contemplate balance, pedal speed, or how to stop; you simply ride and get to enjoy the experience without thinking one bit about the mechanics you have committed to muscle memory.

That is the power of knowledge and experience – you gain confidence and the ability to grasp all that is going on around you. And while you cannot always speed up experience, which is a product of time, you can accelerate your knowledge by continually choosing to maintain and develop your skill sets and talents, better preparing and equipping yourself for the work you do. If you are new in your current role, hang in there and seize opportunities to master the skill sets you can, knowing that time and experience will be on your side in a few months!

Your ability to work well and to be a resource for and leader of others is directly related to your confidence in your abilities and the knowledge you can nurture, enhance, and develop by *choosing to own your development.*

I vividly remember my Army Special Forces drill sergeant commanding over us at airborne paratrooper training:

"There are two kinds of people in this world, the quick and the dead! And since none of you look dead, you better get moving!"

And many years later a similar message in the words of Mark Kay Ash:

"There are three types of people in this world:
  those who make things happen,
  those who watch things happen,
  and those who wonder what happened."

Both messages planted in me rules I firmly follow: *In order to keep living I need to move!* and *Leaders are the ones who MAKE THINGS HAPPEN, starting with me MAKING THINGS HAPPEN for me.*

To maximize your impact and influence as an effective leader, choose to embrace development as your lifeline. Because you are reading this book, you care about having impact. You know you can positively influence your colleagues and your company. You know you are a leader and you want to maximize your effectiveness. Thank you for caring!

With the fast pace at which companies are growing today, you might find yourself in a leadership role even though you have limited formal experience or training. And you probably work for people who have various degrees of experience and training and are faced with the challenges that come with that. Regardless of your position or role, your commitment to grow impacts those around you, so stay the course! Commit to being great at your job and learning all you can in order to be confident and resourceful. This alone allows you to be strong for others and frees you to lead positively right where you are.

Choose What Skills to Develop

Choosing what skills to develop and how to focus your growth is an exciting opportunity. There are countless universal skills you can learn to augment your abilities, and there are industry-specific and job-specific skill sets to continually be training in and maintaining.

For example, in the world of medical devices that I come from, a regulatory affairs specialist needs to continually stay up to date on regulations, modifications, and appropriate protocols; a marketing specialist benefits from being on the cutting edge of social media, digital advertising, and creative messaging; while a nutritionist should be current on diet trends to be able to advise clients knowledgably. But what else would be good to develop?

As part of a course titled "Navigating Your Career and Taking Control of Your Future" I had the opportunity to present to a diverse group of twenty-four men and women who worked in STEM-related roles. Some were just starting their post-collegiate careers and others had been in their careers for twenty years or more. Their common interests revolved around how best to maximize their career opportunities moving forward, both in their current roles and in preparation for future roles. To initiate the program I posed the following question:

> "True or False: You are where you are today because of the choices you made yesterday, and the day before, and the day before...."

After they contemplated and discussed their answers, I posed the question:

"What choices can you make today to better navigate where you land tomorrow?"

I divided them into three groups and they were to brainstorm answers to the following additional questions:

"What skill sets do you need to do well at your current level at your current job?"

"What skill sets would help you be better prepared to take on the next level or job you might like to explore?"

Before you review their answers, take some time to reflect on and record your own answers to these questions.

Reflection Exercise 34

Take time to assess your current choices and skill sets and their impacts on achieving your future goals.

Download the Journal at: www.leadershipbychoice.com

Here's what they came up with:

Group A – Current
- Interpersonal/Relationships
- Technical: polymer knowledge, statistical analytics, NPD/PMO
- Adaptability/Flexibility
- Time management
- Accountability
- Regulatory/Compliance
- Problem-solver
- Organizational
- Leadership/Team-building
- Motivation
- Ongoing education

Group A – Future
- Project management
- Education
- Leadership
- Accountability
- Problem-solving
- Networking/Relationship-building
- Creativity
- Experience/Perspective
- Technical
- Flexibility/Adaptability
- Technical skills/Budgets
- Assertiveness (Confidence)/Self-awareness

Group B – Current
- Interpersonal
- Problem-solving
- Negotiating skills
- Current software
- General processes
- Conflict resolution
- Organization
- Presentation skills

Group B – Future
- Opportunity
- Broadening horizons
- Strategic thinking/Understanding of business strategy
- Strong technical skills
- Have a broad network/Connections
- Attitude
- Sales

Group C – Combined Lists

- Computer skills
- Analytical skills
- Communication
- Writing
- Risks
- Interpersonal
- Listening
- Budget management
- Time
- Problem-solving
- Negotiations
- Decision-making
- Mentorship
- Building a Team
- Leadership/Motivation
- Organizational skills
- Confidence
- Proactive
- Science knowledge
- Objectivity
- Compromise
- Presentation skills
- Creativity
- Accountability-you & others
- Influence & sales
- Flexibility
- Trust
- Passion
- Critiquing
- Certification/Education
- Business presence

As you review the lists you may notice the following common themes and noted areas for development that appeared for both current and future jobs:

- Interpersonal skills
- Leadership and Team-building
- Problem-solving
- Networking/Making connections/Mentoring
- Organization and Time management

- Negotiation skills

- Sales skills

- Budget management

- Technical skills/Computer skills

- Analytical skills

- Confidence/Self-awareness

- Adaptability/Flexibility

- Presentation/Communication skills

Independent of the job-specific data and training, the above lists contain common skill sets and functions that cross-pollinate all disciplines, jobs, companies, and roles. These skills help you in your current role and simultaneously position you for future opportunities.

Schedule Time for Development

If you can attend professional courses or training, do so. However, you have other options at your fingertips. There are endless choices for training on the internet such as webcasts, podcasts, digital books, audio books, webinars – the list of resources is unlimited. It is up to you to choose what you want to focus on developing and then determine how best to achieve it. If you work in an organization that supports your development, even better. Your organization might assist you in setting up your training or even sponsor training for a group of you who would all benefit from additional training on a similar topic. But if not, that should not stop or slow you down in establishing your personal development plan. Make it a priority and schedule time for development on a regular basis.

Consider embracing opportunities for the members of your team as well, regardless of your organization's formal succession planning. For example, you could take the lead and coordinate monthly training opportunities on different topics. Each month could highlight a specific skill set, featuring different people with diverse strengths to lead the training. While it can be nice to bring in outside talent for more formal training, often people with the needed skills already work in your team. This is a great way to develop presentation skills, collaboration, and teamwork while simultaneously learning and developing.

A Word on Succession Planning

I have to admit I feel a little naive in sharing this with you, but it wasn't until recently when I was preparing to teach a workshop on succession planning with a group of new managers that I discovered the true meaning of the term. Wikipedia defines it this way:

> Succession planning is a process for identifying and developing new leaders who can replace old leaders when they leave, retire or die. Succession planning increases the availability of experienced and capable employees who are prepared to assume these roles as they become available.

I always considered professional development to be synonymous with succession planning. I didn't view my development as a strategic initiative for the company, and always felt grateful that my manager and company were investing in me and supporting my development. Regardless of whether or not my manager was investing in my development for the strategic future planning of the company or for my personal development, the message I received was clearly that my company *cared* about me. And for that reason my loyalty and dedication to the organization grew and I was eager to do my best, no longer just for me but also for the very people and company that were supporting me.

Development Objectives

For as long as I can remember, in addition to having quarterly sales goals and forecasts to achieve I also had two development objectives that I was equally responsible to work towards. It was part of the culture I was fortunate to have experienced early in my professional career. During every field visit with my manager – a quarterly event in which he shadowed me for two days – we reviewed performance goals, objectives, and my developmental progress in these two areas. At the end of the two days I received a written "Field Visit Letter" documenting the topics we reviewed, performance measurements, and goals and objectives for the upcoming weeks. For me this was just how it was done; it was what I adopted as the norm. And as a result I assumed everyone had developmental objectives and benefitted from clearly articulated strategies and performance feedback.

In later years, when I moved into formal management roles, I continued this system of reviewing quarterly objectives, providing feedback, and establishing one or two developmental areas to help each team member excel at their current role and prepare for their future roles. I enjoyed being a part of their journeys as they continually improved. Having experienced managers who invested deeply in me early in my career, I came to appreciate people as the single most valuable resource a company has. I firmly believe that investing in people is not only the right thing to do but is a strategic imperative.

In every company there is attrition – the turnover or loss of employees. The loss of good, productive, contributing people hurts an organization. In addition to the personal element of losing a valued friend, colleague, or leader, there is a negative financial impact – a result of lost productivity during the time of vacancy from the position: finding, hiring, and training a replacement; and the transition time it takes for the incumbent to become a fully contributing employee. There is a domino effect felt throughout an organization when a positive and influential person leaves. Research on exit interviews and conversations with departing employees indicated that losing good people was often directly related to their immediate supervisor. People stay in a job they are less than enchanted with as long as they connect with and like their supervisor, and people leave jobs they love when they are not aligned with their supervisor.

Going back to the speed at which companies are growing today, it is very likely that a large percentage of managers are leading teams having had little or no training in leadership. For those of you in this very position, own your leadership development and consider acquiring the following skill sets to positively impact your effectiveness with your immediate teams:

- Dynamic communication and presentation

- Delivering performance feedback

- Conducting performance reviews

- Setting up SMART goals (specific, measurable, achievable, realistic, time-based)

- Situational leadership

- Team-building

- How to motivate and inspire a team

- How to build trust and collaboration

- Effective negotiating

- Interviewing and hiring

- Human resource management

- Problem-solving

- Time management

- Sales 101 – understanding the sales process

- How to develop a strategic plan

With people as your number one resource, development of first-line managers is invaluable. If you are that manager, own your development so you can quickly build your skills and confidence to be the leader you want to be. Having experienced the rich rewards of being both the young employee early in my career and the seasoned manager building and developing the next generation of leaders, I believe the benefits of creating a culture of development were as evident years ago as they are today. Investing in the development of your people is not only a great thing to do, but is also strategic and provides a significant return on your investment. Some of the benefits of developing people include:

- Builds a well-educated and highly functioning team

- Demonstrates your commitment to your employees

- Fosters loyalty from employees

- Improves retention of employees

- Feeds succession planning

- Attracts highly driven and talented employees

- Constantly pushes you and your team to stay current with practices, models, and strategies

- Improves morale, confidence, trust, and overall teamwork

When You Invest in You, You Invest in Others

This is an investment in their future and an investment in the productivity and performance of your organization. You are facilitating their ability to grow and develop greater confidence in their work. Giving people opportunities to learn and take on more responsibility gives them a sense of pride and confidence that only experiencing it can.

You can create this culture and influence change by modeling leadership and leading by example even if you are not in a leadership role. No matter your current position, create your own development, share it with others, and encourage others to do the same. You don't have to possess any of the skill sets discussed above to guide others towards development; just fostering a culture of continued growth is a step in the right direction. You don't have to provide the training per se; just support their efforts. Consider turning any opportunity for development into a team initiative and work side by side on objectives. You can draw from the lists provided above or create your own.

Earlier I asked if you would work for you. Here I ask you to be your own manager and invest in your growth as if it is your top strategic investment. That requires that you do for yourself what you would do for a team member reporting to you:

- Assess your strengths.

- Understand your weaknesses.

- Identify your current job performance and areas for improvement.

- Review goals and aspirations for the next level of work.

- Review gaps in your skill sets in your current role and your future role.

- Identify opportunities for development and strategies for implementing them.

- Set up a plan for one or two development objectives.

- Establish accountability metrics for quarterly review.

When you create development objectives, consider what you've done to develop yourself in the past, examine your present skill set, and think about the roles you are interested in for the future and how soon you need to prepare for them as you identify skills that will best support your growth. Take into account your preferred learning style and your strengths.

The Past: Strengths and Experiences
Take a moment to reflect on how you got where you are today. Think about your education, training, and skill set. Honestly acknowledge the skills, strengths, and experiences that led you to your current position.

Fill in the blank: The choices I made "yesterday," such as_____ , contributed to where I am today. Note how you feel about where you are today.

Reflection Exercise 35

Explore what has contributed to your success and achievement to date.

Download the Journal at: www.leadershipbychoice.com

The Present: Add to Your Current Skill Set

Identify one or two skills in your current role you can develop now to help you do your job better. Take time to honestly review how you could improve the work you do now.

Reflection Exercise 36

Identify specific areas in which you can improve your current work performance.

Download the Journal at: www.leadershipbychoice.com

The Future: New or Expanded Roles

You might already know what new job or additional responsibilities you want to take on based on the vision you worked on earlier in the book. What additional skill sets or training would be required? Identify one or two ways to engage in such development now.

Using my development objectives below as examples, create your own based on the skills you want to gain for your current and future roles. Take your objectives to your current supervisor or a trusted colleague for review and discussion. They might have valuable feedback to consider even if your company will not be involved in your development and doesn't have such an initiative available. Sharing your desire and commitment can inspire others to do the same – *leadership by choice* in action.

Sample Development Objectives

Early in my sales career in 1995 I decided I really wanted to lead a sales team, but I had a lot yet to learn. My professional development objectives were a combination of one that would help me do better in my existing role and one to help me develop towards leadership:

1. Learn to manage priorities – I worked closely with my manager to do a better job at prioritizing daily tasks because I wasn't always achieving top priorities.

2. Improve in preparing written feedback – As a sales trainer I was responsible for preparing written follow-up documentation accounting for the strengths and development areas of my trainees. Improving this skill was part of my training in preparation for taking a management role.

Now, in 2018, my professional development objectives are:

1. Improve my public speaking and social media presence – Much of my work requires presentations and speaking; my desire is to continually learn how to create impactful presentation techniques for both in-person and social-media delivery.

2. Learn how to develop and implement web-based training – Clients continue to ask if I offer my programs online, so one area of focus is to develop a web-based platform that meets the needs of leaders globally.

Personal Development Objectives Are Still Learning
If you can't decide what areas to focus on, choose one or two things you are simply excited to learn about! They don't even have to be related to your current field of endeavor. Embrace the opportunity to be challenged, move forward, and make it happen. Remember the words of my drill sergeant: "If you aren't moving you must be dead." Stay alive! Have some fun and make a list of ten things you have always wanted to do or learn that aren't work-related. Call it a bucket list. You will be amazed by how invigorating it can be to experience something new. Adding a new hobby or interest to your life indirectly helps your performance and confidence at work.

I grew up just outside Boston, and later I drove on Storrow Drive every morning, watching the Harvard Crew Team row. Loving the water and being an early riser, I often imagined how amazing it must feel to be out on the Charles River at the crack of dawn, rowing on the still waters. So in the summer of 2017 I decided to join a "learn to row" program on Lake Quinsigamond in Worcester, Massachusetts. I felt bold doing something I had always thought looked like fun – empowered, crazy, who knows, I was learning something new, interacting with a group of strangers, and yes, rowing on a dew-covered, perfectly still body of water as the sun crested at 5:30 in the morning. It was a "pinch me" moment as I realized it wasn't a dream and I was really rowing! I was doing something I had only dreamed of, completely for me and not work-related – or so I thought!

As I embraced the sport, I infused myself by listening to *The Boys in the Boat* by Daniel James Brown on CD, and experienced pure humility at the complexity of the sport. I couldn't help but relate my experience to the work I do. I was experiencing the essence of this chapter. It felt wonderful to learn and master something new. There is a sense of pride, accomplishment, and confidence that the process of being a student and learning fuels. The lessons, pearls of wisdom, epiphanies, and correlations I experienced while learning rowing are now ingrained in the work I do with executive teams – an unexpected yet welcomed byproduct!

Embrace learning and the confidence that added knowledge can provide. Choose to own your development and you are leading by choice.

Reflection Exercise 38

APPLICATION: Review your professional and personal development opportunities. Identify two development objectives. How do you plan to implement these objectives moving forward? How will this improve your ability to maximize your impact and influence as a leader?

Download the Journal at: www.leadershipbychoice.com

CHAPTER 6

Praise People on Purpose

People crave recognition! There, I said it! And I will say it again: People crave recognition in the workplace! It goes a long way, and originates from a heart of gratitude. If you want to have impact and influence, embody this, breathe this, live this.

One of the single leading contributors to job dissatisfaction is feeling underappreciated. And it doesn't apply only to those seeking awards and accolades. Everyone wants to feel that their work is recognized and appreciated. To a certain degree it validates what they do, why they do what they do, and the hours they invest doing it.

Early in this book I noted that professionals spend on average 75 percent of their waking hours working, and you might fall into this category. You are hardworking and highly dedicated to your work. It is completely understandable that you want to be appreciated at times and recognized for the amount of time, effort, contribution, and emotional energy you invest in the work you do each day.

So I challenge you to be the very leader you would want to work for by choosing to embrace the concept of praise and recognition right now. You don't need a fancy title to do this, nor do you need a big desk or even an office. And if you have all of that, it doesn't make you weak or less of a leader to take the time to praise and acknowledge others. In the eyes of someone receiving praise and recognition, it's not "fluff"! This simple act gives you an immediate opportunity to create positive change for others even if you do not feel the need to receive praise.

One little dose of positive affirmation and genuine recognition fuels the anabolic energy and attitude discussed in chapter 3, opening up space for broader creative and impactful thinking! If each of your co-workers functioned at high levels of energy and attitude, triggered in part by praise and recognition you provided, imagine the thoughtful creativity that could be unleashed. Consider the competitive advantage your team might gain.

When you lift other people up, you shift their energy. When you shift their energy, they now have the opportunity to maximize their performance and who they are as people and professionals. When people show up to meetings eager to interact and engage with open minds, they are primed to create greater opportunities and solutions. And as I wrote above, you do not need a title to do this. You are impacting transformation right where you are by the very nature of your interaction and the praise and recognition you choose to deliver.

If it's that easy, that simple, why is it so difficult for us to do – myself included? Sometimes I am so driven by the goal that I forget to slow down and recognize and appreciate simple yet worthy contributions.

Mary Kay Ash, founder of Mary Kay Cosmetics and a visionary beyond her time, built a multibillion-dollar company, still in business today, with one of the founding principles being the power of praising people to success. She challenged her employees and consultants to imagine that everyone they met, came in contact with, or passed by was wearing an invisible sign around their neck that said "Make me feel important," and to never forget this when working with people. I encourage you to adopt this thinking for just one day and see if it just might be a great idea for every day.

Praise need not be a large celebration or involve lengthy preparation. When it comes from the heart – from a genuine grateful attitude – it becomes part of who you are. You start to see people and actions differently. You become authentically grateful for even mundane daily tasks. You can simply praise or express sincere thanks to the custodial worker in the bathroom you use daily, or the clerk at the drive-through window who serves you coffee each morning. Take note of their name on their uniform and say, "Julie, every day I use this bathroom and every day you clean it. Thank you! Thank you for the work you do and how you contribute to this company. You provide me with a clean bathroom, and while it may go unnoticed, you are making a difference to me and I appreciate you!" Or when you get your coffee, ask, "May I ask your name? I just want you to know that I see you almost every morning and have never thanked you for the smile you share at the start of my day. I really appreciate it, and you, and wanted to be sure you know that you make a difference to me and are important!"

Trust me and try it. Both of those conversations were real for me and both yielded really special results. Not only did the recipients appreciate the effort and words, but I felt great doing it, and now have two new friends, always eager to support me. Try it and see what happens for you. (Although, if you have teenagers, be prepared for them to think you are a bit nutty – I'm hoping it will be a life lesson they later embrace for themselves!)

Being able to praise and recognize freely and authentically comes from developing genuine gratitude and thankfulness in your heart. One way to do this is to consciously reflect on all you are thankful for. It's helpful at first to establish a certain time each day to do this, like first thing in the morning or last thing before falling off to sleep. The best way to make it a habit is to create a gratitude journal.

Gratitude Journal

At the same time each day, so it's part of a routine, write in a notebook or your favorite device three things you're thankful for that occurred that day, or the day before if you do this in the morning. The key is to do this daily for a period of time. It is believed that it takes about twenty-one days of consistent behavior to establish a habit. When you maintain a gratitude journal you experience a calming transformation in your life. I found that making my journal entries in the evening just before going to sleep creates a calming shift in my brain and allows me to put the many topics running circles in my brain to rest and peacefully transition into a deep and easy sleep.

One Thanksgiving season our church congregation tried this very exercise with a slightly different twist you might enjoy: Each week we chose a different area of focus, and we couldn't name the same thing more than once. One way to do this in your journal is to choose categories of importance to you. They can be reflective of your core values, work-related topics, or a combination of topics. For example, consider any of the following prompts for your journal:

- Today I am grateful for the following three things:

- I am grateful for (name of specific family member) because s/he:

- I am thankful for (name of person at work) because s/he:

- I am thankful that I have a family that:

- What I love most about the life I live is:

- I appreciate my work for the following three reasons:

- I am thankful that my manager is:

- What I value most about the work I do is:

- I am thankful for my gifts of:

- I am thankful for technology/music/art, as it provides:

- I am grateful for my home because:

Reflection Exercise 39

Explore your thoughts and experiences with *recognition.*
Create a gratitude journal.

Download the Journal at: www.leadershipbychoice.com

Share Your Gratitude

Feel free to explore additional prompts, as these are only a few to get you started. As you journal about the people you are thankful for, consider sharing this exercise with them and revealing your gratitude towards them and why you are grateful. Even if it seems trivial, take time to share it with them. For example, I work with an incredibly talented website developer who is responsive and easy to communicate with. Despite speaking with her weekly about a variety of projects, I recently made it a point to cease our usual project-related dialogue to simply thank her and let her know how much I value the work she does and the working relationship we have developed over the past two years. It's one of my journal entries, so I realized it had been a while since I communicated this with her and appreciated having a prompt to do so.

As you reflect on the people and things you are most grateful for, you might notice your values reflected in how you appreciate others. By openly praising someone directly you are also communicating your values and reinforcing actions that are important to you. This helps you subconsciously reinforce actions you want repeated – efforts that support the growth, direction, vision, and values you most resonate with. Recognize them, call attention to them, praise them! I know you know this already, but it is often the mistakes, flaws, and misses that scream for your attention, not just with others but also in how you assess yourself. Focus on the positive behaviors and patterns supporting direction and growth.

How to Give Praise and Recognition

Be specific, being sure to name the act and acknowledge the result of the act. For example:

- "Thank you, John, for showing up at the meeting prepared and on time. As a result we were able to get through the agenda efficiently and had a productive meeting that moved us closer to our goal this month. I appreciate that you value our meeting time and that you do what needs to be done to prepare for it. I know it might seem as if this is part of doing your job, nonetheless I still want you to know that I appreciate your work and it does not go unnoticed."

- "Thank you, Jaime, for keeping a positive attitude. No matter how difficult the day is, you show up at work with a smile on your face and a willingness to work. It might be who you are, it might be what you do, but it makes a difference here in the office by keeping energy high, which we need these days, so thank you."

- "Pat, I know closing the quarter has meant arduous and long hours. I know the time it has taken away from your family. I want you to know that I appreciate your dedication and hard work to wrap everything up. I also don't expect you to sustain these hours all the time. Please schedule a day to take some down time with family or whatever you need, and consider it my way of saying thank you."

- "Kris, I know this merger and transition has had its challenges. Your leadership with your team during this time has been exceptional. You have been able to keep them inspired and focused on the goal when I know many might be questioning the future. Thank you for your ability to keep a clear vision in front of them and for maintaining sales and productivity throughout."

- "Nick, I wanted to thank you for putting together the recent professional development meeting for us. Despite your busy schedule running and overseeing the company, I appreciate and respect that you continue to support our growth and development. I continue to learn a lot from you as our leader."

These are one-on-one interactions that go a long way.

Celebrate and Have Fun!

Don't be afraid to have fun! Consider holding monthly or quarterly team meetings (or when the moment calls for them) to recognize those who report directly to you, your colleagues, and your peers in front of each other. Even if you are not the formal leader, you might be surprised by how well this is received. Recognition should not be limited to formal occasions.

When I worked as vice president of sales and marketing at a small start-up company of six, we always found time to celebrate our successes no matter how large or small. It kept us going and it made us laugh. I felt it was my job to make sure I acknowledged good work for the company. The CEO didn't tell me to do this, nor did anyone else, but I wanted to have fun with it. There was no budget for plaques or gifts, but with company letterhead and fat-tipped, multicolored markers I was able to create meaningful paper tributes, and that was all that was needed.

One of our engineers, Bryan, spent hours on the road driving endless miles delivering parts and products to the manufacturing facility to ensure we got our preliminary products made. At the same time he developed diverticulitis, necessitating emergency surgery. All went well, and Bryan was the first and only proud recipient of a hand-drawn "Busted Gut Award" for "going the extra mile!"

I share this with you to remind you that the size of your team or budget doesn't matter. You can have fun with recognition with a bit of creativity. Awards do not need to have a large monetary value to mean something. It is through the words and the sincerity of the recognition that someone feels appreciated. Almost five years later, Bryan shared that he still has his hand-drawn Busted Gut Award proudly displayed in his home office. We still reminisce about our days working together, and would welcome any opportunity to work together in the future. The power of recognition and praise goes a long way and it doesn't need to cost a lot of money or take a lot of time. I encourage you to do this regardless of your title or position, right where you are.

Reflection Exercise 40

APPLICATION:
Practice maintaining your gratitude journal and
offering recognition for 28 days.
Identify a fun activity for your team.
Make notes about your experience and
what results you observe.
Share your results.

Download the Journal at: www.leadershipbychoice.com

CHAPTER 7

Listen to Hear

Surely you've heard the expression *You have two ears and one mouth; use them proportionately: listen twice as much as you speak.* But why is it so difficult to do? What makes listening so difficult, both in business and in our personal lives? Is it ego? The desire to be seen as having all the answers? Do we just like to hear our own voices? Do we think that finishing others' sentences demonstrates "like" thinking? Does speaking over others to provide a solution demonstrate competence? Knowledge? Professionalism?

Maybe we just share a universal desire to be heard; which is why listening is such a powerful and effective way to maximize your impact as a leader. With the intrinsic desire everyone has to be heard, there is not a lot of room for listening, is there?

You can change that right now, and choose to listen. Choose to acknowledge the value of *listening to hear* rather than with the intention of providing a well-articulated response.

In chapter 5 I shared that it was only when I gained greater confidence through experience and training that I was able to relax in my dialogue with clients, listen, and really hear the needs they were revealing versus pretending to listen while actually thinking my own thoughts and trying to formulate my answers.

My hope is that throughout *Leadership By Choice* you have been building your confidence about the person you are and the leader you are choosing to be. When you are confident and at peace with who you are as a leader – *the very unique and perfectly designed you*, aligned with your values, and tracking with a crystal-clear vision – then and only then can you truly move towards listening to hear yourself as well as others.

Listening to hear others requires you to cultivate a genuine curiosity and a desire to honor what they have to say and let it sink in before responding. Listening to hear yourself requires taking time for quiet reflection, knowing that there is an incredible power inside you and that only by being calm and silent can you feel it and hear it.

Listen to Hear Others

Be curious. Take the time to ask people about themselves. Ask them what they dream about doing some day. Ask them what they are currently working on. Ask them what gets in their way or holds them back. Ask them what they struggle with. Ask them how you might be able to better support them. Ask genuine, open-ended questions, and then be quiet. Listen. Hear.

Don't anticipate their answer. Focus on their words, and listen. If their answer requires a response, there is no need to rush it. It's perfectly okay not to respond right away. What you are communicating is that you are listening to them, and the value of that goes much further than immediately providing your two cents. If that seems awkward, explain that you will respond after you've thought through what they had to say. The value of listening and giving them the opportunity to communicate and be heard surpasses any response you might have.

People want to be heard. Your co-workers want to be heard. It often doesn't matter whether you agree with them or not, they just want have a chance to share their ideas, thoughts, opinions, and concerns.

In my work a common theme comes up: the constant feeling of not being heard or appreciated. Everyone has a voice. And everyone has thoughts. On one level this seems so simple and so obvious, but the problem is that we are all seeking to be heard at the same time. Stepping on each other's words can negatively impact a relationship, and being a leader entails nurturing relationships, not shortchanging them. As inspirational author Andy Stanley pointed out, "Leaders who don't listen will eventually be surrounded by people who have nothing to say."

Your strength as a leader lies in the strength of the team and people around you, so you can't afford not to hear from them! Their thoughts, input, and opinions are valuable sources of information. You want to provide opportunities for them to be heard and make yourself available so you can gather the valuable information that fuels your organization and the people working in it. Listening to what they have to say – and to what they don't say – offers you perspective and informs you about the environment your team functions in. When people can come to you and know they will be heard, they trust you.

Develop Active-Listening Skills

Think of someone you feel completely open and comfortable talking with – someone you know will listen to you and will make you feel heard. What is it about how they listen that makes you feel that way? Most likely they shared eye contact and gave you the sense they were listening only to you by not glancing around the room, at their phone, or at their computer. They probably nodded and offered you verbal and non-verbal cues that they were listening, and ultimately provided their undivided attention. Take note of your current active-listening habits and consider refining them as needed in the following ways:

- Practice eye contact when engaged in a conversation. Resist the temptation to glance at your watch, clock, phone, or computer while in conversation.

- Practice finding comfort in the silent communication, pauses, and thinking that happens when someone is deep in discussion and thought. In other words, just because there is a pause or silence, don't feel the need to say something simply to break the silence. Allow the other person time to process their next thoughts.

- Intentionally demonstrate your desire to be present at the beginning of a conversation by closing your laptop, closing the door to your office, or suggesting moving to where there is no noise or distraction so that you can be fully present.

- If you are having the conversation on the phone, follow the same practices: close your computer, move to where you can focus and listen, and remove distractions. Just as when the other person can see you, openly say, "Give me a moment to [move away from my desk/into a more private area] so I can give you my undivided attention."

With that very effort of evaluating and refining your active-listening skills you are choosing to lead. You will have immediate impact in your workplace, *today*, by making this change.

Of course it's not easy to just suddenly become a good listener. [Gulp] I must come clean – I am not very good at this at home. My husband, Tom, could easily fill you in, for a small fee…

While I know that listening comes from a deep and genuine curiosity, and that authentic listening is about listening to hear without having an answer, I also have a deep and genuine passion for problem-solving. That should not be my excuse, but I have conflicting values that struggle for dominance when I'm conversing with someone: listening to hear, and problem-solving.

I am an analytical person (remember I was a math major?), and I love solving puzzles! Sudoku, Unblock Me, Tetris, logic puzzles… I am addicted. And I constantly need to remind myself that conversations with my husband are not puzzle-games, despite my treating them that way at times. I have been accused of trying to complete his sentences (stepping on his words) and answering the question I thought he was intending to ask instead of the one he did (discomfort with silence).

He's right. Guilty as charged. Of course, I counter that it is not that I don't want to listen, or don't care to hear what he's saying – it's just that I love puzzles. I find it sort of fun to anticipate what the rest of his sentence or thought is. After all, isn't that showing that he and I are connected deeply; that I know his thoughts and words? Not so... oops! It truly is horrifically rude and doesn't bode well for our marriage. It's interesting that even though I'm aware that I do this, I still do it anyway. My problem-solving zeal is so much a part of me that I have to work at undoing it in these moments.

Power of Three

All kidding aside, improving your listening skills might require some additional tools. One technique I use when working with new sales representatives is applicable to everyone. I encourage new sales representatives to embrace the "power of three." When they meet with clients and are working to understand their needs, I challenge them to hold back from sharing anything about what they're selling until they have asked three open-ended questions and heard the answers to each.

Why three? First of all, it slows you down, suppressing the need to immediately answer the first inquisition, and forces you to seek greater understanding. Otherwise you run the risk of regurgitating features and benefits about what you're selling that might have nothing to do with the client's ultimate interests. Second, it keeps you focused on the client and really understanding what they're seeking. Third, it's an opportunity to think and not be quick to answer, which allows you to become curious and hear them on a deeper level. Laying this groundwork helps you effectively respond to their needs.

While this is a technique I have used with salespeople, the benefits are the same no matter what type of work you do. By preparing and asking three open-ended questions, you truly elicit a deeper understanding of the other person's needs, concerns, desires, and motivation. Your curiosity and willingness to listen lets the other person know you care.

Reflection Exercise 41

Identify three people you are genuinely curious to learn more about.
What are three open-ended questions you can ask that will initiate genuine, authentic conversations with others?

Download the Journal at: www.leadershipbychoice.com

Listen to Hear Yourself

How often is the answer you seek already within you, but you are too busy to listen for it? The process for transforming this problem is the same as it is for listening to others – taking the time to inquire and listen! When faced with uncertainty, get to the heart of what you already know. You are the expert on you. No one knows you better than you. You and you alone are uniquely qualified to be you, to advise you, and to direct your path.

I first saw the cartoon above years ago. I loved it then, while working in sales and marketing, and I love it even more today by replacing "see any crazy salesmen" to "take time to slow down and think." It reminds me how frequently in my career I have internally said (and felt and lived), "Slow down?! How can I slow down – I have too much to do to slow down!" It also reminds me of another mantra I learned from my amazing, eighty-eight-year-old, self-employed father, who still works full time in his law office: "Sleep?! I will sleep when I am dead – right now I still have a lot to accomplish." And posted on a tired piece of paper on the wall behind his desk is this Calvin and Hobbes cartoon by Bill Watterson:

**GOD PUT ME ON EARTH TO
ACCOMPLISH A CERTAIN NUMBER
OF THINGS. RIGHT NOW I AM SO
FAR BEHIND, I WILL NEVER DIE.**

Making Time to Think

Despite growing up in an environment that supported relentless hours of work, at some point along the way I came to accept that slowing down and taking time to sleep can enhance productivity and efficiency and actually help me achieve more. I continue to be amazed that your brain works continuously even while you sleep. On countless mornings I have risen with solutions and creative ideas packaged nicely with a bow, answers to challenges from the previous day. In college I studied "unsolvable" math problems for hours, only to awaken with knowledge of the one step I'd been missing in my calculations and a sudden answer to the problem. Learn to appreciate the magnitude of the knowledge and ability you possess, and choose to provide a clear and quiet space to access it.

With smart phones and 24/7 access to the world, clearing time to quiet down and think is more challenging than ever. Many professionals who travel sometimes relish that twenty minutes at the beginning and end of a flight when they have to switch their phones to airplane mode and stow their laptops. Add some noise-blocking headphones and you can actually experience two twenty-minute segments of time with no access to or interruptions from the world. Ahhhh... silence! Such a treasured time – a gift of sorts! If it's so cherished and coveted, why is it so difficult to intentionally schedule this time into each and every day? Even twenty minutes?

The fear of missing out, or F.O.M.O. as my teenagers call it – of not immediately reading and responding to an email, text, or phone call – has become a way of life. We have grown into a society in which immediate gratification and communication is the norm and anything short of that is unacceptable. Simultaneously we have grown to rely on searching the web (or asking "Alexa" to do so) rather than using our own brains and knowledge.

Not only do you expect quick turnaround in communication from others, but you also hold yourself accountable for the same. Even when you choose to take some time for reflection, thinking, or strategic planning, your phone is within reach and not on airplane mode. While you are thinking, those rings and vibrations are subtly in the background, usually resulting in at least a quick glance to gauge the urgency of the communication. *Regardless of the message, it interrupts your thinking.* Time is a limited resource. **Taking time to think and reflect may be your single most important strategic investment in yourself, both professionally and personally. Invest in that time, void of distractions, as wisely as possible.**

Reflection Exercise 42

Implement a strategy to create regular, dedicated time to hear *you*.

Download the Journal at: www.leadershipbychoice.com

In a recent coaching call with a senior executive in a fast-growing IT company, he was reflecting on our work and the strides he felt he was making. As he spoke I could hear a totally different person with a new energy and excitement for his work and his role as a leader. Just weeks earlier I had observed and experienced his deep turmoil and conflict regarding his working relationship with a colleague. And I wasn't alone. Others had noticed and commented on the constant friction between the two. Hours were being consumed in meetings as the two debated topics, even ones they had debated the day or week before. Some in the room would sit idly waiting to see where the day's debate would land, while others shifted to their laptops to catch up on email or other more pressing matters.

As an observer I couldn't help but notice that despite the apparent impasse, they were on the same side of the debate, but they couldn't hear each other.

In the coaching call I acknowledged the transformation I was hearing from him, and he shared that he had taken time to reflect on the situation. He made a choice to listen to his colleague with curiosity and less judgment and interpretation. He was choosing to *listen to hear* and not with the goal of responding simply to have an answer or win the conversation. His new positive attitude was screaming through the phone. With this choice alone he created transformation.

After a pause, smiling through the phone (yes, you can hear a smile) he said, "Oh, and by the way, my wife wanted me to be sure to tell you one more thing during our call today."

"What's that?" I asked.

"I started meditating." Silence.

"And?" I asked.

"Well, I really think that by taking time to be quiet each day I have been better able to process my growth, the work we are doing together, and the direction I want to go. It is *really* helping, and I think it is as important, and maybe more so, to my progress."

Regardless of the other person's position in your organization, when you slow down and really listen it allows them to feel heard, and when they feel heard they in turn are more content to sit back and truly listen as well.

Only One Minute

It had been a few months prior that I introduced the value of taking time to be quiet with a client in one of my workshops. As I do with other groups, I introduced a one-minute exercise based on one at LiveStrong.com that I found to be provocative:

> For one minute, close your eyes and breathe deeply. Breathe into your belly, below your ribs. If you have difficulty doing this while sitting, find a flat surface to lie on. Place your right hand on your belly, and your left hand over your chest. As you inhale, feel your hand

rise with your belly while trying to keep your chest and left hand from rising. Inhale and exhale with equal timing. (Deeper, fuller "stomach breathing" is beneficial for the entire body as it opens the blood vessels deep in the lungs to allow more space for oxygen to enter the blood and improves concentration and mental capacity.) (LiveStrong.com https://www.livestrong. com/article/310564-chest-vs-stomach-breathing)

Take a moment and try it yourself. How did it feel? It can be pretty surprising how one short minute of breathing can clear your mind and allow room to think, reflect, create, or problem-solve. By bringing oxygen-rich blood cells to your brain, core, and entire body, tension is released, opening up avenues for creativity and thought.

One single minute of stopping to breathe allows you to pause, regroup, and move along in your day, your decision-making, and your leadership. If the thought of meditating or creating quiet time for reflection to clear your mind is a new concept for you or you can't imagine having enough time, one minute – sixty little seconds – is an incredibly worthwhile baby step you can easily incorporate into your daily routine, as my client has now discovered.

Taking time to breathe allows you to step back, clear your head, listen to yourself, sort through issues, and relax. If one minute can do all that, imagine the power of taking more time to listen within. How you do it is your choice. Many get their quiet time while exercising; others use various forms of meditation, prayer, or a combination of the two.

Multitasking Can Add Power

A few years ago I decided to multitask my quiet time. I wanted to exercise – or I should say I felt the *need* to exercise – and I also felt the desire to commit more deeply to my faith journey. So I started to walk thirty minutes each day while listening to *Your Move* by Andy Stanley, a thirty-minute podcast series I found incredibly educational, funny, inspiring, and uplifting. It was amazing how grounded and energized I became in those thirty minutes. I couldn't wait to get out of bed to put my earbuds in and my sneakers on! It was transformational to start my days off by clearing my brain and getting aligned with my core values. My walking progressed to running, and my faith grew stronger. The ideas and creativity that come from this morning ritual are endless.

If you're not regularly taking time to listen to yourself, try some different ways to do so and find one that works for you. Consider exercise, getting outside, meditation, prayer, yoga, or driving – yes, for some driving is when their brains kick into gear. Some people download guided meditations to their favorite device. A friend of mine listens to calming, directed breathing meditations in bed before going to sleep. As one who suffers from insomnia, this has afforded her the ability to transition into a deep sleep, clearing her brain in the process. It works tremendously well for her.

Meditation

By definition, "Meditation is a precise technique for resting the mind and attaining a state of consciousness that is totally different from the normal waking state. It is the means for fathoming all the levels of ourselves and finally experiencing the center of consciousness within. Meditation is not a part of any religion; it is a science, which means that the process of meditation follows a particular order, has definite principles, and produces results that can be verified." ("What Is Meditation," Yoga International, https://yogainternational.com/article/view/the-real-meaning-of-meditation)

There is a lot of information available if you are interested in meditation. Some of my colleagues have found that they like using guided meditation and breathing apps they download to their phones. Others access various videos on meditation. Some have discovered a variety of mind exercises to clear the brain and stimulate thought. I recently started using an app called MindPT, which includes a series of photographs accompanied by music specifically designed to soothe and focus the brain. I like this app so much that I am in the process of creating one to support this very book!

Needless to say, there are many resources at your fingertips. Find one that works for you and schedule time daily to shift your brain from the everyday workload to a few minutes of separation. The space you create will open up your ability to listen to yourself – to hear yourself. And in so doing, your confidence and leadership qualities will continue to expand, allowing you to maximize your impact and influence on those around you, in the workplace, today – right where you are!

Change of Scenery

Sometimes it helps to get away from it all. While establishing a daily routine that enables you to shift and clear your mind is helpful, occasionally you might feel the need to go away to a program or retreat designed to accommodate this very practice. It can be a great way to spend time either alone or in the company of other professionals in an environment conducive to getting quiet; hearing yourself; and designing, creating, and connecting to your vision, values, and energy towards building the culture or team you desire to lead.

This can also be a great way to bring a team together at an offsite meeting designed for reflection, think time, and strategic planning. As a facilitator of and participant in offsite meetings and retreats designed for both corporate teams and individuals, I have witnessed the power of deliberately taking time to change your environment, slow down, and access and focus on the tremendous creativity, ideas, and wisdom you possess that are just waiting to help you achieve your goals. The choice is yours.

Reflection Exercise 43

If you could choose any environment that would maximize your ability to think, plan, strategize, and create, what would it look like?

Download the Journal at: www.leadershipbychoice.com

To maximize your impact and influence in your workplace, today, right where you are, choose to take time to be quiet, reflect on your core values, align your vision, engage your energy, embrace your barriers, feed your development, ignite your gratitude, and hear all you have inside of you – your uniquely and perfectly designed you.

Reflection Exercise 44

APPLICATION: Schedule time to review your reflections from this book. As you read your responses, what do you hear about yourself? What opportunities exist today for you to have greater impact and influence as a leader?

Download the Journal at: www.leadershipbychoice.com

PART III

The Action:
Embrace the Impact

You are a force
Filled with unique energy
Put into motion by your activity
Creating momentum in those around you
Transferring energy
Resulting in activity of others
Building greater momentum in all directions
Creating positive action and equally positive reactions
You are the impact
You are the influence
You are making a difference
And it started with one action
It started with you

Your Leadership Matters

Embrace the Journey!

This is *your* chapter of *Leadership By Choice*. Now that you have reflected on values, vision, energy, barriers, development, praise, and listening, what do they mean to you? There was a reason you chose this book. My guess is because you, too, want to make a difference and know you have so much inside of you to offer. So what is it? What is the difference you want to make? And most important, what does it mean to *embrace the journey*?

Please document your vision for your impact and influence and what embracing the journey means to you, and please share it with me if you're inspired to do so, as there is nothing that makes me happier than hearing about others' leadership journeys.

Thank you for taking the time to journey through this book with me. My vision is for everyone to love their work, embrace their ability to lead, and have impact and influence in the workplace. And now it is up to you to make this happen. You have the knowledge, the power, and the attitude to create a positive change in your workplace right now. I believe in my heart that you chose this book because you already know this! Now go do it! And do it with an energy, excitement, commitment, and vision that can only come from you.

Imagine each ball in Newton's Cradle initiating its own sequence and transfer of force, momentum, and action. While your impact is only partially visible, each ball or person you impact in turn propels a brand new sequence, creating an infinite cycle of action and reaction. Everything you do has tremendous influence. Embrace this concept. Seize your presence and opportunity. *Choose to make a difference where you are – there is a reason you are there.*

Regardless of where you want to be in the future, you are somewhere now, and that somewhere needs *you*. It is in the now that you can lead, inspire, and positively impact the daily working lives of others. Thank you for caring to do so, and for embracing the honor and privilege associated with being that very person – that leader – who is bold enough and courageous enough to step up and positively lead, and do so from the role you occupy today!

To maximize your impact and influence in your workplace, today, right where you are, choose to be the leader that only you can be.

Reflection Exercise 45

APPLICATION: Reflect on your journey as a leader and the impact you choose to have, today.

Download the Journal at: www.leadershipbychoice.com

ACKNOWLEDGMENTS

Writing this book has truly been a journey. For years I have been developing thoughts and processes, eager to share them in some capacity. Biting the bullet and really going for it has been nothing short of an amazing experience, and one I certainly could not have done alone. I am humbled and in awe of the many people along the way who supported me and encouraged me.

I would like to acknowledge God for placing this vision in my heart, inspiring me, guiding me, and filling me with knowledge and grace, daily; for His son, Jesus Christ, for providing me with a living example of the ultimate transformational leader, teaching, guiding, mentoring, listening, loving, accepting, forgiving, and empowering others with candor and humility; and for the Holy Spirit for feeding my quest to be faithful and fearless on a daily basis.

I would like to acknowledge my amazingly supportive husband, Tom, for always being there to lift me up, pick me up, and walk beside me over the past twenty-two years. As a third grade teacher he has personally touched the lives of hundreds of children and families directly in his classroom and indirectly in the many programs he created to ignite a passion for learning, growth, and development. As the students and families continue to reach out, some now twenty years later, sharing their successes and appreciation for their third grade experience and all they are doing in the world now as adults, I am simply amazed by the impact and influence my husband has had as a leader.

I would like to acknowledge our beautiful teenagers, Carolyn, Nicholas, and Jordan, who continue to teach me and inspire me to constantly grow and be better for them. Words are not enough to express my passionate love and appreciation for each of them for giving me the humbling honor and title "Mom."

I would like to acknowledge my parents, Karnig and Carol, married for fifty years, for instilling in me a work ethic like none-other and for teaching me that I could do anything I put my mind to. And my siblings, Charlie, Eddie, and Karen, for teaching me about the strength of family, love and unconditional support. You are each so amazing and I cherish the laughter we have shared.

To my confidant and best friend, Gina, I thank you for always being there, for your listening ears, the early morning and late night phone calls, your support and encouragement – I am so grateful for your cheerleading and belief in me every step of the way.

ACKNOWLEDGMENTS

I would also like to acknowledge the network of inspiration and support that brought this book together: Christine, Carrie, Ranilo, and Gwen – for accepting my insane desire to pull this off in a few months and for rallying to inspire, mentor, and guide me along the way; and my clients, colleagues and friends, far too many to list, who openly shared their hearts and challenges with me, many noted in this book, giving me the humble opportunity to learn and grow from you and be your coach, mentor, and friend.

From the bottom of my heart, thank you!

AN INVITATION TO
THE READER

One of the most challenging pieces of writing this book has been accepting that your journey through the material would be independent of "live" interaction as typically happens during my in-person workshops and programs. Hopefully, you took the time to download the *Reflection Journal* to enhance your experience reading the book, and shared it with a friend or two. If not, you can still do that!

As an additional resource, I designed an accompanying interactive, live webinar series to support each chapter, providing the opportunity for group training and interaction on these very topics. If you would like to participate or be informed of upcoming programs, please connect with me at **www.leadershipbychoice.com** and I will be sure to keep you abreast of the logistics, webinars, and retreats in which a deeper dive into the very topics of this book are addressed in a group fashion.

Furthermore, if other areas of interest came up for you as you read the book that are challenging you or you are craving more work around, please email me and let me know about it! I truly want to hear from you and support you however I can.

From my heart, thank you!

Reflection Exercise 46

INVITATION:
**Connect with me and share your top three
takeaways from this book!
If you found this book helpful and want to encourage
others to embrace their leadership, please
consider reviewing my book on Amazon at www.
leadershipbychoice.com**

Download the Journal at: www.leadershipbychoice.com

REFERENCES AND INSPIRATIONS

Life Application Study Bible, New Living Translation, Tyndale House Publishers, Inc.

The 7 Habits of Highly Effective People by Stephen Covey

Awaken the Giant Within by Tony Robbins

Boys in the Boat by Daniel James Brown

Energy Leadership by Bruce D. Schneider

How to Stop Worrying and Start Living by Dale Carnegie

How to Win Friends and Influence People by Dale Carnegie

Mary Kay by Mary Kay Ash

HBR's 10 Must Reads on Managing Yourself, Harvard Business Review

Start With Why by Simon Sinek

Success One Day at a Time by John C. Maxwell

TGIF: Today God Is First (a daily inspiration blog), Volume 1, Os Hillman

The Five Dysfunctions of a Team by Patrick Lencioni

The Power of Focus by Jack Canfield, Mark Victor Hanson, and Les Hewitt

The Power of Positive Thinking by Norman Vincent Peale

The Purpose Driven Life by Rick Warren

Unbroken by Laura Hillenbrand

You Are Special by Max Lucado

Your Move, podcast series by Andy Stanley

ABOUT THE AUTHOR

Sue Salvemini is the founder and president of Focal Pointe Consulting Group, Inc., a company dedicated to developing exceptional leadership teams and bringing passion and energy into the workplace at every level. With over twenty-five years of corporate and military experience developing leaders, building teams, and launching medical device products and businesses, Sue founded her company to honor her greatest values of leadership and to create a company positioned to empower others to embrace their visions and live their legacies through meaningful work.

Sue's passion and commitment to leaders and organizations is reflected in her coaching, speaking, workshops, and writing. As an executive coach and speaker, she works with individuals and teams, helping them develop their authentic leadership styles to maximize their positive impact on the people and organizations they serve. She works with CEOs and executive leaders creating customized workshops and programs specifically in alignment with the company vision and mission. Her ability to customize her programs yields a diverse array of clients including a mix of Fortune 500 companies, ground-level start-up companies, nonprofit organizations, and individual philanthropists and business owners.

Sue holds a Bachelor of Science Degree in Mathematics from the University of Massachusetts and a Master of Education Degree in Human Resources and Organizational Change from Boston University. She is an Institute of Professional Excellence in Coaching Certified Professional Coach and an International Coach Federation Associate Certified Coach. She is a certified Energy Leadership™ Index Master Practitioner and has worked extensively with Myers Briggs™, DISC™, Situational Leadership™, and Patrick Lencioni's Five Dysfunctions of a Team models. Sue's diverse experience in sales, marketing, and product development provides her with appreciation and understanding from multiple perspectives, roles, and responsibilities.

When not conducting workshops, consulting on business strategy, or coaching high-performing executives, Sue is at her home in Massachusetts playing a good game of gin rummy with her husband of twenty years, Tom; thoroughly engaged with their three teenagers, Jordan, Nicholas, and Carolyn; or hopping into an occasional Tough Mudder or half marathon for the exercise and fun of it.

To learn more about Sue and Focal Pointe Consulting Group, Inc., please visit **www.focalpointeinc.com.**

Made in the USA
San Bernardino, CA
29 November 2018